ESPECIALLY FOR

....

FROM

....

DATE

....

Devotional Inspiration
from *A Christmas Carol*
by Charles Dickens

God Bless Us
Every One!

ANNIE TIPTON

BARBOUR BOOKS
An Imprint of Barbour Publishing, Inc.

© 2016 by Barbour Publishing, Inc.

Print ISBN 978-1-63409-891-5

eBook Editions:
Adobe Digital Edition (.epub) 978-1-63409-986-8
Kindle and MobiPocket Edition (.prc) 978-1-63409-987-5

All rights reserved. No part of this publication may be reproduced or transmitted for commercial purposes, except for brief quotations in printed reviews, without written permission of the publisher.

Churches and other noncommercial interests may reproduce portions of this book without the express written permission of Barbour Publishing, provided that the text does not exceed 500 words or 5 percent of the entire book, whichever is less, and that the text is not material quoted from another publisher. When reproducing text from this book, include the following credit line: "From *God Bless Us Every One!*, published by Barbour Publishing, Inc. Used by permission."

Scripture quotations marked NIV are taken from the HOLY BIBLE, NEW INTERNATIONAL VERSION®. NIV®. Copyright © 1973, 1978, 1984, 2011 by Biblica, Inc.™ Used by permission. All rights reserved worldwide.

Scripture quotations marked NLV are taken from the New Life Version copyright © 1969 and 2003. Used by permission of Barbour Publishing, Inc., Uhrichsville, Ohio, 44683. All rights reserved.

Scripture quotations marked NLT are taken from the *Holy Bible.* New Living Translation copyright© 1996, 2004, 2007 by Tyndale House Foundation. Used by permission of Tyndale House Publishers, Inc. Carol Stream, Illinois 60188. All rights reserved.

Parts of this book is based on a work of fiction. Names, characters, places, and incidents are either products of the authors' imaginations or used fictitiously. Any similarity to actual people, organizations, and/or events is purely coincidental.

Cover photo © Lebrecht Authors/Lebrecht Music & Arts/Corbis

Published by Barbour Books, an imprint of Barbour Publishing, Inc., P.O. Box 719, Uhrichsville, Ohio 44683, www.barbourbooks.com

Our mission is to publish and distribute inspirational products offering exceptional value and biblical encouragement to the masses.

 Member of the
Evangelical Christian
Publishers Association

Printed in China.

ontents

Introduction

Charles Dickens knew how to tell a good tale. By the 1840s he was an established author, world famous for his characters and plotlines. But even as he enjoyed his successes, the plight of the poor was always heavy on his heart. When Dickens was a young man, he saw his father locked up in debtors' prison, and he was forced into employment at the age of twelve in a shoe polish factory. Thus Dickens wove the theme of poverty—especially child poverty—into many of his stories, including *David Copperfield*, *Oliver Twist*, and others.

As Dickens began work on a new Christmas story in 1843, he seized the opportunity to write something more than a feel-good tale. *A Christmas Carol* would be an instrument for change that could spur readers into action to help those in need. He poured his heart and soul into the story, making Scrooge, Bob Cratchit, Tiny Tim, Fred, and the rest some of the most memorable characters in literature.

After the nativity story, there may be no other holiday story more beloved than *A Christmas Carol*. Dickens's novella has been adapted into countless movies, radio dramas, stage productions, and dramatic readings for the past century and a half. The bestselling story (now in the public domain) has been in print continually since its first publication. Although the story has no overt Christian message, we can glean many inspirational spiritual lessons from the pages—and this devotional includes fifty-two of them. From redemption and forgiveness to generosity and kindness, many of the themes in the book line up perfectly with scripture, specifically with Christ's teachings.

At the beginning of each devotional reading in this book, you will find an excerpted passage from the original Dickens story, followed by a bit of my own imaginings surrounding the story (apologies to Mr. Dickens) and an inspirational thought that puts the scene into context from a biblical perspective. You may find that you would like to read the entire story alongside this devotional (I recommend it, in fact!). If you don't own a copy of *A Christmas Carol*, don't fret. The full text can easily be found online, both as text and as audiobooks.

This Christmas, and many Christmases to come, it's my prayer that you and your family can draw new inspiration from Dickens's wonderful story. God bless us, every one!

Merry Christmas!
Annie Tipton

Stave One

SCROOGE'S HEART OF COLD

Oh, but he was a tight-fisted hand at the grindstone, Scrooge! A squeezing, wrenching, grasping, scraping, clutching, covetous old sinner! Hard and sharp as flint, from which no steel had ever struck out generous fire, secret, and self-contained, and solitary as an oyster. The cold within him froze his old features, nipped his pointed nose, shriveled his cheek, stiffened his gait, made his eyes red, his thin lips blue, and spoke out shrewdly in his grating voice. A frosty rime was on his head, and on his eyebrows, and his wiry chin. He carried his own low temperature always about with him; he iced his office in the dog days; and didn't thaw it one degree at Christmas.

External heat and cold had little influence on Scrooge. No warmth could warm, no wintry weather chill him. No wind that blew was bitterer than he, no falling snow was more intent upon its purpose, no pelting rain less open to entreaty. Foul weather didn't know where to have him. The heaviest rain and snow and hail and sleet could boast of the advantage over him in only one respect. They often "came down" handsomely, and Scrooge never did.

Ebenezer Scrooge is not a nice man. Call him what you want: grouch, party pooper, old grump, stinker, killjoy, jerk. He is not just having a bad day—he is having a bad life. And he seems to do his very best to make everyone around him as miserable as possible, too. Scrooge would do well to listen to Mom's advice that if you don't have anything nice to say, then don't say anything at all. Scrooge with his icy demeanor freezes the warmth out of any situation, even a joyous holiday celebration. He has something close to an evil superpower.

Here in the first description of the main character of our story, we don't learn the full extent of his miserly, greedy ways. We don't learn about his lack of interpersonal skills or the fact that he despises Christmas. Instead, we learn that he is a cold, hard man who would like nothing more than to be left alone. How cold is he? He is so cold that he acts as his own personal air conditioner in the summer and Deepfreeze in the winter. Scrooge is so stuck in his arctic ways that it seems the only way this frigid man will experience a thaw is with help from others. (We'll get to that later.)

But as the oyster he is, ol' Ebenezer won't let anyone close enough even to *try* to help him. In fact, Scrooge thinks he is fine just the way he is, so why would he need help from anyone, anyway?

Most people are easy to love, and those are the folks we choose to be around every day. But Jesus calls us to love the Ebenezer Scrooges in our lives. Showing love to these unlovable stinkers doesn't always feel nice, but Jesus is very clear in what He tells us in Luke 6:32–33, 35 (NLV):

> "If you love those who love you, what pay can you expect from that? Sinners also love those who love them. If you do good to those who do good to you, what pay can you expect from that? Sinners also do good to those who do good to them. . . . But love those who hate you. Do good

to them. Let them use your things and do not expect
something back. Your reward will be much. You will be
the children of the Most High. He is kind to those who
are not thankful and to those who are full of sin."

Why does Jesus teach us to love our Scrooges? Because
He loves us despite the fact that we are stinkers, too. We
don't deserve the gift of God's Son coming to earth as a
baby that night in Bethlehem. We don't deserve Jesus'
sacrifice of allowing Himself to be killed on the cross in
our place. We do not deserve God's love and forgiveness
and gift of salvation. We don't deserve any of it, but we are
immeasurably thankful for it.

Who are the Scrooges in your life? Ask God to open your
heart to ways to love these people. Keep your eyes and ears
open to opportunities to share Jesus' love in practical ways.

My children, let us not love with words or in talk only.
Let us love by what we do and in truth.
1 John 3:18 nlv

TOO BUSY FOR CHRISTMAS

*Once upon a time—of all the good days in the
year, on Christmas Eve—old Scrooge sat busy in his
countinghouse. It was cold, bleak, biting weather,
foggy withal, and he could hear the people in the court
outside go wheezing up and down, beating their hands
upon their breasts, and stamping their feet upon the
pavement stones to warm them. The city clocks had only
just gone three, but it was quite dark already—it had
not been light all day—and candles were flaring in the
windows of the neighboring offices, like ruddy smears
upon the palpable brown air. The fog came pouring in
at every chink and keyhole, and was so dense without,
that, although the court was of the narrowest, the
houses opposite were mere phantoms. To see the dingy
cloud come drooping down, obscuring everything, one
might have thought that Nature lived hard by, and was
brewing on a large scale.*

Scrooge is a busy man. Busy getting on with his cold,
hard, solitary life. He is an exceptional worker—
has been his whole life—and silly things like Christmas
are nothing but a distraction from getting on with the
importance of his work.

Christmas Eve is the same as any other day to Ebenezer,
and the dank, dark London winter is no cause for a festive
mood. If anything, the weather affirms Scrooge's state of
mind. So he continues counting his money, tallying the

profits in an accounting ledger with a tiny stub of a pencil as wispy fingers of fog creep through the keyhole of his office door. It doesn't matter. Nothing matters but the task in front of him.

It's easy to pity Scrooge in this scene. Although we don't read any description of holiday festivities or merrymaking, we do know that it's Christmas Eve. Perhaps a street or two away, tiny shops are already filled with last-minute errand runners. A bell choir may be ringing in the joy of the holiday, and a group of grubby street children may be singing a slightly off-tune rendition of "Good King Wenceslas" with the hopes of collecting a shilling in their caps. And Scrooge is oblivious to the possibility of it all—shoulders slumped over his desk, head down, squinting at the column of numbers that doesn't quite add up.

What does your daily life look like? Are you and your family suffering from jam-packed schedules, and are those schedules even tighter November through January? Between work, school, sports, clubs, hobbies, special performances, volunteering, caroling, baking, shopping, wrapping, cleaning, decorating, and partying, your holiday to-do list may seem like the never-gets-done list.

Although we probably don't want to identify ourselves as Scrooges, we may find that we have more in common with him than we think. Scrooge is so caught up in his own work that the joy of Christmas is passing him by. Granted, Scrooge has no interest in celebrating Christmas (and you may *love* Christmas), but the result is the same: if our time and attention are so divided between every event and task, the true holiness and meaning of the holiday will pass us by, too.

During Jesus' time on earth, He taught His followers the

importance of rest, and He even modeled a life of rest to His apostles:

> *Then Jesus said, "Let's go off by ourselves to a quiet place and rest awhile." He said this because there were so many people coming and going that Jesus and his apostles didn't even have time to eat. (Mark 6:31 NLT)*

Did you catch that? ". . .Jesus and his apostles didn't even have time to eat." We all have had times when we have been this busy—and Jesus knows exactly what that feels like!

Christmas can be a time of peace and refreshment, but only if we are willing to make rest a priority. That might mean saying no to some of the unimportant voices shouting for your attention. This year make decisions as a family about the most important holiday activities and events, and then agree not to add any more to your schedules once the plan is in place. You might be surprised to find that the most meaningful times of the season are often the simplest ones.

> *Truly my soul finds rest in God; my salvation comes from him. Truly he is my rock and my salvation; he is my fortress, I will never be shaken.*
> PSALM 62:1–2 NIV

A NEPHEW'S KIND WORDS

"A merry Christmas, uncle! God save you!" cried a cheerful voice. It was the voice of Scrooge's nephew, who came upon him so quickly that this was the first intimation he had of his approach.

"Bah!" said Scrooge. "Humbug!"

He had so heated himself with rapid walking in the fog and frost, this nephew of Scrooge's, that he was all in a glow; his face was ruddy and handsome; his eyes sparkled, and his breath smoked again.

"Christmas a humbug, uncle!" said Scrooge's nephew. "You don't mean that, I am sure?"

"I do," said Scrooge. "Merry Christmas! What right have you to be merry? What reason have you to be merry? You're poor enough."

"Come, then," returned the nephew gaily. "What right have you to be dismal? What reason have you to be morose? You're rich enough."

Scrooge, having no better answer ready on the spur of the moment, said "Bah!" again; and followed it up with "Humbug!" . . .

"Don't be angry, uncle. Come! Dine with us tomorrow!" . . .

"Why did you get married?" said Scrooge.

"Because I fell in love."

"Because you fell in love!" growled Scrooge, as if that were the only one thing in the world more ridiculous than a merry Christmas. "Good afternoon!"

"Nay, uncle, but you never came to see me before that happened. Why give it as a reason for not coming now?"

"Good afternoon," said Scrooge.

"I want nothing from you; I ask nothing of you; why cannot we be friends?"

"Good afternoon!" said Scrooge.

"I am sorry, with all my heart, to find you so resolute. We have never had any quarrel, to which I have been a party. But I have made the trial in homage to Christmas, and I'll keep my Christmas humor to the last. So a merry Christmas, uncle!"

Scrooge has little family left in this world, but his nephew, Fred, enters the Scrooge & Marley office with enough Christmas spirit to spread a glimmer of light in the depressing place. From the moment Fred bursts through the front door, it's obvious he is a young man full of joy. And not just because it's December twenty-fourth. No, Fred is a man who lives with a song perpetually in his heart, a smile on his lips, and a twinkle in his eye.

The kind of person Ebenezer Scrooge despises.

Uncle Ebbie's unwelcoming grumblings and humbugs to Fred's greetings are nothing new to Fred—his mother's only brother never had a good word to say to anyone, Christmas or not. And even though Fred knows Scrooge will turn him down just as he does every year, nephew extends to uncle an invitation for Christmas dinner at the home he shares with his wife.

Scrooge jumps at the opportunity to change the subject and take a jab at his nephew. "Why did you get married?" (In other words: "Wives cost too much money and are a waste of time. Yours is no exception, nephew!")

Still, Fred speaks kindly to his old uncle, and even when Scrooge repeatedly dismisses him from the office, Fred continues to return kind words, reason, and Christmas joy. Try as he might, Scrooge simply cannot snuff out the Christmas candle inside Fred's heart.

Responding with loving words when we encounter hateful or mean language and attitudes is not easy. Sometimes, especially at Christmas, it may even be the people we love and care for who say things that hurt us:

> *"When are you going to find that special someone and settle down?"*
> *"You know, next year would probably be a good one to lose that weight you keep saying you want to lose."*
> *"Isn't it about time for you two to start having kids?"*
> *"I simply can't stand people who would vote for that candidate."*

Although spending time with family during Christmas is a blessing, there are times when personalities clash and relationships can be strained. What difficult topics or conversations do you know will come up during celebrations with family or friends? How can you steer the conversation in a more positive and uplifting way, rather than falling into the trap of retaliating with hurtful words?

Want some guidance from God's Word? Here is what Ephesians 4:29 (NLT) says about the words we use:

> *Let everything you say be good and helpful, so that your words will be an encouragement to those who hear them.*

Words are powerful tools that can be used as either demolition equipment to tear down or bricks to build up. Scrooge is the foreman of the demo crew, and Fred is a master bricklayer. This Christmas choose to follow Fred's lead with kind words that encourage others.

A gentle answer turns away anger, but a sharp word causes anger. The tongue of the wise uses much learning in a good way, but the mouth of fools speaks in a foolish way. . . . A gentle tongue is a tree of life, but a sinful tongue crushes the spirit.
PROVERBS 15:1–2, 4 NLV

THE TWO GENTLEMEN

They were portly gentlemen, pleasant to behold, and now stood with their hats off, in Scrooge's office. They had books and papers in their hands, and bowed to him. . . .

"At this festive season of the year, Mr. Scrooge," said the gentleman, taking up a pen, "it is more than usually desirable that we should make some slight provision for the poor and destitute, who suffer greatly at the present time. Many thousands are in want of common necessaries; hundreds of thousands are in want of common comforts, sir."

"Are there no prisons?" asked Scrooge.

"Plenty of prisons," said the gentleman, laying down the pen again.

"And the Union workhouses?" demanded Scrooge. "Are they still in operation?"

"They are. Still," returned the gentleman, "I wish I could say they were not.". . .

"Oh! I was afraid, from what you said at first, that something had occurred to stop them in their useful course," said Scrooge. "I'm very glad to hear it."

"Under the impression that they scarcely furnish Christian cheer of mind or body to the multitude," returned the gentleman, "a few of us are endeavoring to raise a fund to buy the poor some meat and drink, and means of warmth. We choose this time, because it is a time, of all others, when Want is keenly felt, and Abundance rejoices. What shall I put you down for?"

"Nothing!" Scrooge replied.

"You wish to be anonymous?"

"I wish to be left alone," said Scrooge. "Since you ask me what I wish, gentlemen, that is my answer. I don't make merry myself at Christmas, and I can't afford to make idle people merry. I help to support the establishments I have mentioned—they cost enough; and those who are badly off must go there."

"Many can't go there; and many would rather die."

"If they would rather die," said Scrooge, "they had better do it, and decrease the surplus population."

It seems that Christmas Eve is going to be nothing but one long interruption to Ebenezer's work, because as soon as his nephew, Fred, leaves, two gentlemen enter the office with one goal in mind: to secure a donation for the poor from the firm of Scrooge & Marley. These two well-meaning men have spent the day talking to businessmen, and every conversation has ended in donations of varying sizes. After all, it is Christmas Eve—a time when most people open their wallets and give.

But Ebenezer Scrooge isn't *most people*.

When the gentlemen state the purpose for their visit, Scrooge responds in a way that, to him, seems very logical. Since he already pays taxes to fund the government-run prisons and workhouses, the needy should go there.

The wide-eyed surprise on the gentlemen's faces gives Scrooge a bit of a jolt. Maybe they'd never thought of such a novel idea! This exchange is his favorite one to have with charity workers. He knew what was coming next: "Not everyone can take advantage of those services, Mr. Scrooge, and many would rather die!"

A malicious twinkle pierces Scrooge's eyes as he utters a response that has taken a lifetime of coldhearted selfishness to craft. "If they would rather die, they had better do it, and decrease the surplus population."

You're a mean one, Mr. Scrooge. Look up *scrooge* in the dictionary, and you will see that this fictional character has his very own entry: "a mean person who is usually stingy with money." A miser, cheapskate, penny-pincher, skinflint, tightwad. Although being responsible with money is a good thing, being a scrooge is something entirely different.

It's easy to fall into the trap of selfishness when it comes to money. After all, we work hard to earn money, so why should we give it to others—especially when we think they might not deserve it?

The truth is that it's important to realize that *our* money is not really *ours*. God owns everything, and He allows us to manage His wealth. Truly living out God's plans for His money means using our resources to show His love to people who do not have as much as we have. When we do this, we are showing that we love God, too.

Jesus explains this in the parable of the sheep and the goats in Matthew 25:34–40 (NLV):

> "Then the King will say to those on His right side,
> 'Come, you who have been called by My Father. Come
> into the holy nation that has been made ready for you
> before the world was made. For I was hungry and you
> gave Me food to eat. I was thirsty and you gave Me
> water to drink. I was a stranger and you gave Me a
> room. I had no clothes and you gave Me clothes to wear.

*I was sick and you cared for Me. I was in prison and
you came to see Me.'*

*"Then those that are right with God will say, 'Lord,
when did we see You hungry and feed You? When did we
see You thirsty and give You a drink? When did we see
You a stranger and give You a room? When did we see
You had no clothes and we gave You clothes? And when
did we see You sick or in prison and we came to You?'
Then the King will say, 'For sure, I tell you, because you
did it to one of the least of My brothers, you have done it
to Me.' "*

This Christmas ask God to show you specific
opportunities for giving, then open your eyes and ears for
those opportunities. That may mean setting aside money
that is intended for the purpose of blessing others in need,
whether locally, regionally, or globally.

*You must each decide in your heart how much to give.
And don't give reluctantly or in response to pressure.
"For God loves a person who gives cheerfully."*
2 Corinthians 9:7 nlt

THE HUMBLE BOB CRATCHIT

Scrooge had a very small fire, but the clerk's fire was so very much smaller that it looked like one coal. But he couldn't replenish it, for Scrooge kept the coal box in his own room; and so surely as the clerk came in with the shovel, the master predicted that it would be necessary for them to part. Wherefore the clerk put on his white comforter and tried to warm himself at the candle; in which effort, not being a man of strong imagination, he failed. . . .

At length the hour of shutting up the countinghouse arrived. With an ill will, Scrooge dismounted from his stool and tacitly admitted the fact to the expectant clerk in the tank, who instantly snuffed his candle out and put on his hat. "You'll want all day tomorrow, I suppose?" said Scrooge. "If quite convenient, sir." "It's not convenient," said Scrooge, "and it's not fair. If I was to stop half a crown for it, you'd think yourself ill used, I'll be bound?"

The clerk smiled faintly.

"And yet," said Scrooge, "you don't think me ill used when I pay a day's wages for no work."

The clerk observed that it was only once a year.

"A poor excuse for picking a man's pocket every twenty-fifth of December!" said Scrooge, buttoning his greatcoat to the chin. "But I suppose you must have the whole day. Be here all the earlier next morning."

The clerk promised that he would; and Scrooge walked out with a growl.

ob Cratchit's mother taught him the value of hard work. And she also taught him never to complain. So even when he can't feel his fingertips, nose, and toes as he diligently completes his work as a clerk at the firm of Scrooge & Marley, he rubs his palms together above the candle at his desk and pulls his threadbare jacket a little more snuggly around his chest. He is thankful for his job. He can provide for his wife and children, and they have a joy-filled life. Of course, there is nothing extra for frivolity, but the Cratchits always make up for it with love.

Except. . .it *would* help to have a bit extra for doctors' bills for the little one. He has looked paler lately, and despite the tiny crutch that Bob fashioned (quite expertly) with a tree limb they found at the park, the boy's limp seems to be getting worse.

Still, there are others much worse off than the Cratchits, so Bob will press on, doing his best for Mr. Scrooge.

As we first meet Bob Cratchit, it's easy to look at him through our modern-day eyes and wonder why he doesn't stand up for himself. He should demand a warmer work environment! Higher pay! Holidays, health care, and a 401(k)! But Bob's circumstances are different than many of ours, and it may be that his position as Scrooge's clerk is the best job he can get. With little to no education, Bob likely worked his way up from a lower-paying job that had even worse or dangerous conditions. A nine-to-five job with steady work and pay that allows him to be home for Mrs. Cratchit's evening meal every night may be Bob's definition of perfect employment.

Scrooge's clerk is a gentle spirit. Unassuming, kind, peaceable, and meek, he returns Fred's Christmas greetings when Scrooge's nephew visits the office. And Bob gently convinces Scrooge to close the office on Christmas Day when the curmudgeonly boss nearly ruins the entire holiday by expecting Bob to work the next day.

Jesus Himself praised and blessed many of the characteristics Bob Cratchit exhibits in His Sermon on the Mount in Matthew 5:5, 8–10 (NLT):

> *"God blesses those who are humble, for they will inherit the whole earth. . . . God blesses those whose hearts are pure, for they will see God. God blesses those who work for peace, for they will be called the children of God. God blesses those who are persecuted for doing right, for the Kingdom of Heaven is theirs."*

Humility flies in the face of the Scrooges of the world, and humbling ourselves and propping others up to be better than ourselves—to have a heart that is pure for others—is a life that pleases God. It's easy to make Christmas a time all about ourselves, but this Christmas take the time to look outward. It may be as simple as letting a frazzled holiday shopper step in line ahead of you at the checkout or offering a smile and a heartfelt "Can I help you with something?" to a coworker, classmate, or family member who looks like he or she could use an extra hand. Humble yourself and watch God work through you!

> *Since God chose you to be the holy people he loves, you must clothe yourselves with tenderhearted mercy, kindness, humility, gentleness, and patience.*
> COLOSSIANS 3:12 NLT

THE LONDON FOG

Meanwhile the fog and darkness thickened so that people ran about with flaring links, proffering their services to go before horses in carriages, and conduct them on their way. The ancient tower of a church, whose gruff old bell was always peeping slyly down at Scrooge out of a gothic window in the wall, became invisible, and struck the hours and quarters in the clouds, with tremulous vibrations afterward, as if its teeth were chattering in its frozen head up there. The cold became intense. In the main street, at the corner of the court, some laborers were repairing the gas pipes, and had lighted a great fire in a brazier, round which a party of ragged men and boys were gathered, warming their hands and winking their eyes before the blaze, in rapture. The waterplug being left in solitude, its overflowings suddenly congealed, and turned to misanthropic ice. . . .

Foggier yet, and colder! Piercing, searching, biting cold. If the good Saint Dunstan had but nipped the Evil Spirit's nose with a touch of such weather as that, instead of using his familiar weapons, then, indeed, he would have roared to lusty purpose. The owner of one scant young nose, gnawed and mumbled by the hungry cold as bones are gnawed by dogs, stooped down at Scrooge's keyhole to regale him with a Christmas carol; but at the first sound of God rest you, merry gentleman, May nothing you dismay, Scrooge seized the ruler with such energy of action, that the singer fled in terror, leaving the keyhole to the fog and even more congenial frost.

The London weather mirrors Scrooge's humbug mood as Christmas Eve trudges toward the evening hours. The fog thickens, and the sights of the coming holiday celebration fade in the haze. First to disappear is the church's steeple, and then the cheery shops' lights and decorations are enveloped by earthbound cloud.

And the cold! It's not a festive chill with the hope of a blanket of new snow, but it's the damp sort of freezing that floods your very soul—the kind of cold that makes you wonder if you will ever be warm again.

It's exactly the weather that Scrooge himself would have ordered for Christmas Eve if he could. Misery for everyone!

Even the happiest, most joyful among us suffer from a case of the humbugs every now and then. Those days when our attitude stinks and we suck the joy out of the air. Maybe it's because we woke up on the wrong side of the bed or one bad thing happened that seemed to snowball into a bunch of bad things. Maybe someone says or does something unkind to us, and the fog from that interaction sends us on a one-way ticket to Humbugville. Sometimes we even like to see our personal fog engulf other people, too—just like Scrooge.

Our attitudes are all too often influenced by people and events that we have no control over. But the source of our attitude really begins with our thoughts. God's Word gives us a list of attitude adjusters that are guaranteed to lift the fog and provide peace in Philippians 4:8–9 (NLT):

> *Fix your thoughts on what is true, and honorable, and right, and pure, and lovely, and admirable. Think about things that are excellent and worthy of praise. Keep putting into practice all you learned and received from me—everything you heard from me and saw me doing. Then the God of peace will be with you.*

The secret to this attitude adjustment is making sure that the foundation of these attitude adjusters is already in our hearts before the inevitable fog comes. For example:

What is true: *God loves me so much that He sent Jesus to make a way for me to be with Him forever.* (John 3:16)

What is honorable: *I will think about others before I think about myself.* (Philippians 2:3)

What is right: *I will treat others the way I would like to be treated.* (Matthew 7:12)

What is pure: *Even when I mess up, God is faithful to make my heart clean again.* (Psalm 51:10)

Training your mind to think about these things when the fog rolls in isn't easy. Pray and ask God to remind you of these promises when you feel the chill of a bad attitude creep in. He is faithful to provide the peace you need to live a joy-filled life every day!

Look through me, O God, and know my heart.
Try me and know my thoughts. See if there is any sinful
way in me and lead me in the way that lasts forever.
PSALM 139:23–24 NLV

SCROOGE'S LONELY CHRISTMAS EVE

Scrooge took his melancholy dinner in his usual melancholy tavern; and having read all the newspapers and beguiled the rest of the evening with his banker's book, went home to bed. He lived in chambers which had once belonged to his deceased partner. They were a gloomy suite of rooms, in a lowering pile of building up a yard, where it had so little business to be, that one could scarcely help fancying it must have run there when it was a young house, playing at hide-and-seek with other houses, and have forgotten the way out again. It was old enough now, and dreary enough, for nobody lived in it but Scrooge, the other rooms being all let out as offices. The yard was so dark that even Scrooge, who knew its every stone, was fain to grope with his hands. The fog and frost so hung about the black old gateway of the house, that it seemed as if the Genius of the Weather sat in mournful meditation on the threshold.

Ebenezer goes about his normal routine after the workday ends, as if it were any other day of the year. Christmas Eve—the night the rest of the world awaits with wondrous anticipation—has no effect on Scrooge. He eats dinner. . .alone. Reads his newspapers and goes over his personal accounts. . .alone. And when he has no more excuse to be out, he walks home—a depressing house once owned by his business partner, Jacob Marley, who died seven years ago.

All around him, unseen, the city celebrates. From

individual houses where families gather for food and games to churches where parishioners honor the holy eve, hearts are overflowing with the Christmas spirit. Yet the stone inside Scrooge's chest barely beats as he approaches the darkened house where he lays his head for a few hours each night. He is so lonely that it's nearly unbearable. He just doesn't know it.

Christmas is a time when loneliness can weigh especially heavy on our hearts. It may oppress a widow enduring her first holiday without her beloved husband. Or perhaps an elderly gentleman in assisted living who has no family living nearby. Or a family who has lost a beloved parent and grandparent. It may plague someone going through a difficult diagnosis and treatment or a young couple who has suffered a miscarriage. Or it may overcome someone new to the area who can't make it home for the holiday. These losses can feel new and terrible all over again once the Christmas season arrives.

God created us to be with other people—to have fellowship with others and to form relationships with them. Here is what Ecclesiastes 4:9–12 (NLT) says about that:

> *Two people are better off than one, for they can help each other succeed. If one person falls, the other can reach out and help. But someone who falls alone is in real trouble. Likewise, two people lying close together can keep each other warm. But how can one be warm alone? A person standing alone can be attacked and defeated, but two can stand back-to-back and conquer. Three are even better, for a triple-braided cord is not easily broken.*

Many of us are blessed to be born into families where this fellowship is a natural part of our lives, but God also places special friends and His family—the church—in our lives to encourage and bless each other. Do you know people in your family or in your church family who could use some extra love this year? Nobody should be alone at Christmastime, and maybe God is asking you to be that person's family this year.

Oftentimes, the lonely might also be people who aren't popular. They might even be downright annoying. They might even be as terrible as Ebenezer Scrooge himself. But still, God calls us to reach out to them. To love them. To show them His light and goodness. Just as the angels first shared the good news of Jesus' birth with the smelly outcasts also known as the shepherds, we have many blessings that we can share with people who need them.

"You are the light of the world—like a city on a hilltop that cannot be hidden. No one lights a lamp and then puts it under a basket. Instead, a lamp is placed on a stand, where it gives light to everyone in the house. In the same way, let your good deeds shine out for all to see, so that everyone will praise your heavenly Father."
MATTHEW 5:14–16 NLT

THE PROBLEM OF THE DOOR KNOCKER

Now it is a fact that there was nothing at all particular about the knocker on the door, except that it was very large. It is also a fact that Scrooge had seen it, night and morning, during his whole residence in that place. . . . Let it also be borne in mind that Scrooge had not bestowed one thought on Marley, since his last mention of his seven-years-dead partner that afternoon. And then let any man explain to me, if he can, how it happened that Scrooge, having his key in the lock of the door, saw in the knocker, without its undergoing any intermediate process of change—not a knocker, but Marley's face.

Marley's face. It was not in impenetrable shadow, as the other objects in the yard were, but had a dismal light about it, like a bad lobster in a dark cellar. It was not angry or ferocious, but looked at Scrooge as Marley used to look: with ghostly spectacles turned up on its ghostly forehead. The hair was curiously stirred, as if by breath or hot air; and though the eyes were wide open, they were perfectly motionless. That, and its livid color, made it horrible; but its horror seemed to be in spite of the face, and beyond its control, rather than a part of its own expression.

As Scrooge looked fixedly at this phenomenon, it was a knocker again. . . .

He did pause, with a moment's irresolution, before he shut the door; and he did look cautiously behind it first, as if he half expected to be terrified with the sight of Marley's pigtail sticking out into the hall. But there was nothing on the back of the door, except the screws and nuts that held the knocker on, so he said, "Pooh, pooh!" and closed it with a bang.

Ebenezer Scrooge tries his very best to ignore the fact that tonight—Christmas Eve—is special. For Scrooge, tonight will prove to be unlike any other of his entire miserable life.

But as he slips his key into the lock on the door to his house, he sees something altogether unbelievable: the door's stone knocker has been replaced with the face of his long-dead business partner, Jacob Marley.

Scrooge startles and his heart thuds dully in his chest and ears. He blinks, hoping to reset his vision to reality, but when the door comes back into focus, Marley's wide eyes stare into Scrooge's very soul, sending a shiver down his spine.

Before Scrooge can make sense of what his eyes are telling him, in the next moment, it's a door knocker again. If he hadn't been so certain of what he saw, Scrooge might even think he was a short step from the deep end of sanity.

We're surrounded by warning signs in our everyday lives. From literal warnings like CAUTION: HOT labels on coffee cups to blinking signs that tell us of road construction ahead, we often go through our days heeding these warnings without much thought.

But sometimes warnings are a little more out of the ordinary. Maybe a twinge in our conscience or a conversation with a friend or family member makes us stop and consider a decision we face or something we're doing. Sometimes these warnings can be straight from God Himself. Think of it: God loves us so much that He wants to keep us from decisions or sins that will harm us. He wants the very best for us, and the very best comes from living within His plans.

God can speak to us through the Holy Spirit, too. As Christians, we have the power of God inside of us, and His Spirit can help us know what God wants us to do and warn us if we're heading down a wrong path. Jesus promises this in John 14:26 (NLV), when He tells His disciples:

> *"The Helper is the Holy Spirit. The Father will send Him in My place. He will teach you everything and help you remember everything I have told you."*

Of course, we may want to ignore a warning sign to keep doing what we want to do. We don't know for sure, but Scrooge had probably encountered other warning signs that he had been living a life doomed for destruction well before his encounter with Marley's face. But still, once this warning passed and everything went back to normal, he dismissed it as if nothing had happened.

If we are wise, we *will* heed the warnings that come our way. But how can we hear the Holy Spirit? Pray and ask for a heart that is ready to feel the Spirit move. The Holy Spirit can make God's Word come alive to us and gain new meaning when we spend time reading the Bible. The Spirit can put ideas in our heads and hearts that are good and pleasing to God.

> *If the Holy Spirit is living in us,*
> *let us be led by Him in all things.*
> GALATIANS 5:25 NLV

NOTHING TO FEAR

The sound resounded through the house like thunder. Every room above, and every cask in the wine merchant's cellars below, appeared to have a separate peal of echoes of its own. Scrooge was not a man to be frightened by echoes. He fastened the door and walked across the hall and up the stairs, slowly, too, trimming his candle as he went. . . .

Sitting room, bedroom, lumber room. All as they should be. Nobody under the table, nobody under the sofa; a small fire in the grate; spoon and basin ready; and the little saucepan of gruel (Scrooge had a cold in his head) upon the hob. Nobody under the bed; nobody in the closet; nobody in his dressing gown, which was hanging up in a suspicious attitude against the wall. Lumber room as usual. Old fireguard, old shoes, two fish baskets, washing stand on three legs, and a poker.

Quite satisfied, he closed his door and locked himself in; double-locked himself in, which was not his custom. Thus secured against surprise, he took off his cravat, put on his dressing gown and slippers, and his nightcap, and sat down before the fire to take his gruel.

Scrooge slams the front door as if to show the door knocker just who's in charge, and the resulting boom echoes through the cavernous house. From the basement to the attic, the sound repeats and multiplies in a way that makes Ebenezer all the more annoyed that his own front door spooked him.

Scrooge's normal nightly ritual is to check all the rooms, but tonight he is still a little jittery from Marley's cold stare, so the checks are done a little more carefully—under the furniture and in the best hiding spaces. All clear.

Scrooge's pulse quickens as he sees the manlike figure looming on the wall, but in a moment he realizes it's just the firelight shadow cast by his robe hanging on a hook.

Double locking the bedroom door, Scrooge is finally convinced that there is nothing to be afraid of. . . . Or so he thinks.

What frightens you? What turns your blood to ice and sends your heart beating so hard that it feels like it will jump right out of your chest? Palms sweaty, breathless, mouth dry, and stomach lurching—we have all been there. Whether it's a fear of the dark, snakes, spiders, heights, small spaces, blood, crowds, public speaking, terrorist attacks, or any other rational or irrational fear, everyone deals with this emotion from time to time. Our fears change as we grow and experience new things, but even if we have conquered our fear of what's living under the bed after finding out it was just the family cat playing with dust bunnies, we might currently be afraid of flying after experiencing a terrifying turbulence-filled trip.

Fear can sometimes be a positive emotion, because it can help us avoid danger. Someone afraid of heights will be likely to stay far from the edge of a cliff. But daily fears and anxiety that stay with us for long periods of time can weigh heavily on our spirits and can even have a negative effect on our relationships and health.

Humankind has experienced fear since sin entered the world in the Garden of Eden, so God's Word has much to say on the subject.

1. God promises that He is always with us:

> *"Do not fear, for I am with you; do not be dismayed,*
> *for I am your God. I will strengthen you and help you;*
> *I will uphold you with my righteous right hand."*
> *(Isaiah 41:10 NIV)*

> *"Do not be afraid. For I have bought you and made*
> *you free. I have called you by name. You are Mine!*
> *When you pass through the waters, I will be with you.*
> *When you pass through the rivers, they will not flow*
> *over you. When you walk through the fire, you will not be*
> *burned. The fire will not destroy you. For I am the Lord your*
> *God, the Holy One of Israel, Who saves you. . . . You are of*
> *great worth in My eyes. You are honored and I love you. . . .*
> *Do not fear, for I am with you." (Isaiah 43:1–5 NLV)*

> *"This is my command—be strong and courageous! Do*
> *not be afraid or discouraged. For the LORD your God is*
> *with you wherever you go." (Joshua 1:9 NLT)*

2. God will take our fear away if we let Him:

> *I looked for the Lord, and He answered me. And He*
> *took away all my fears. (Psalm 34:4 NLV)*

> *Give all your worries and cares to God, for he cares*
> *about you. (1 Peter 5:7 NLT)*

3. God has equipped us to conquer fear with His help:

For God has not given us a spirit of fear and timidity,
but of power, love, and self-discipline.
(2 Timothy 1:7 NLT)

I can do all things because Christ gives me the strength.
(Philippians 4:13 NLV)

The real reason not to fear is that God is in control of everything that happens, and that includes every situation, every scenario, *anything* our imagination can think up to scare us. Choose to live in the confidence that God has already conquered every fear you will ever face.

When I am afraid, I put my trust in you.
In God, whose word I praise—in God I trust and
am not afraid. What can mere mortals do to me?
PSALM 56:3–4 NIV

THE DISTRACTION OF WORRY

It was a very low fire indeed; nothing on such a bitter night. He was obliged to sit close to it, and brood over it, before he could extract the least sensation of warmth from such a handful of fuel. The fireplace was an old one, built by some Dutch merchant long ago, and paved all round with quaint Dutch tiles, designed to illustrate the scriptures. There were Cains and Abels, Pharaoh's daughters, Queens of Sheba, angelic messengers descending through the air on clouds like feather beds, Abrahams, Belshazzars, apostles putting off to sea in butter boats, hundreds of figures to attract his thoughts; and yet that face of Marley, seven years dead, came like the ancient prophet's rod, and swallowed up the whole. If each smooth tile had been a blank at first, with power to shape some picture on its surface from the disjointed fragments of his thoughts, there would have been a copy of old Marley's head on every one.

"Humbug!" said Scrooge; and walked across the room.

Ebenezer Scrooge's imagination is running wild. Even though he has already secured the room and locked himself in for the night, he can't get old Jacob Marley's stony door knocker face out of his head.

Scrooge hates the fact that every shadow and odd shape in sight makes him jump. Even the Bible scene carvings around his fireplace seem to take on a strange, eerie look. He has never put any faith in the Bible, but maybe tonight he could take some comfort in scripture. . .if he knew any scripture. *Good heavens, has Abraham's gaze always looked so similar to Marley's piercing stare?*

Have you ever been so distracted, so fixated on something that's worrying you, that you can't seem to focus on what's in front of you? Sometimes our thoughts are so consuming that we have a difficult time talking about, thinking about, or doing anything else but what is related to that worrisome thing.

Worry ties our stomach in knots and keeps us awake at night. We bite our nails and wring our hands and consider the *what-ifs* and *whens* and *hows* and *whys* of all the things in life we often have no control over. We worry about big things (*What if someone in my family gets really sick?*) and trivial things (*What if my phone battery dies before I can find a charger?*) and everything in between. And when we're worrying, it seems like the biggest and most important thing that's ever happened in the history of mankind. We're focused on ourselves and how the outcome could affect us. We're in a cycle of needing control but feeling helpless. And while we worry, we're not focused on our faith.

In Luke 12 Jesus commands us not to worry and goes on to show us examples of how our Father God takes care of His creation:

> *"That is why I tell you not to worry about everyday life—whether you have enough food to eat or enough clothes to wear. For life is more than food, and your body more than clothing. Look at the ravens. They don't plant or harvest or store food in barns, for God feeds them. And you are far more valuable to him than any*

birds! Can all your worries add a single moment to your life? And if worry can't accomplish a little thing like that, what's the use of worrying over bigger things?

"Look at the lilies and how they grow. They don't work or make their clothing, yet Solomon in all his glory was not dressed as beautifully as they are. And if God cares so wonderfully for flowers that are here today and thrown into the fire tomorrow, he will certainly care for you. Why do you have so little faith?

"And don't be concerned about what to eat and what to drink. Don't worry about such things. These things dominate the thoughts of unbelievers all over the world, but your Father already knows your needs. Seek the Kingdom of God above all else, and he will give you everything you need.

"So don't be afraid, little flock. For it gives your Father great happiness to give you the Kingdom." (verses 22–32 NLT)

God has an abundant life planned for us, His beloved children. A life of faith is living in the freedom to embrace all of the blessings and opportunities that our heavenly Father places in our path. Choose to let go of your worry and live the life God wants you to live.

Do not worry. Learn to pray about everything. Give thanks to God as you ask Him for what you need. The peace of God is much greater than the human mind can understand. This peace will keep your hearts and minds through Christ Jesus.
PHILIPPIANS 4:6–7 NLV

JACOB MARLEY'S GHOST

"You are fettered," said Scrooge trembling. "Tell me why?"

"I wear the chain I forged in life," replied the Ghost.
"I made it link by link, and yard by yard; I girded it on
of my own free will, and of my own free will I wore it.
Is its pattern strange to you?"

Scrooge trembled more and more.

"Or would you know," pursued the Ghost, "the
weight and length of the strong coil you bear yourself?
It was full as heavy and as long as this, seven Christmas
Eves ago. You have labored on it, since. It is a ponderous
chain!"

Scrooge glanced about him on the floor, in the
expectation of finding himself surrounded by some fifty
or sixty fathoms of iron cable; but he could see nothing.

"Jacob!" he said imploringly. "Old Jacob Marley, tell
me more! Speak comfort to me, Jacob!"

"I have none to give," the Ghost replied. "It comes
from other regions, Ebenezer Scrooge, and is conveyed by
other ministers, to other kinds of men. Nor can I tell you
what I would. A very little more is all permitted to me.
I cannot rest, I cannot stay, I cannot linger anywhere.
My spirit never walked beyond our countinghouse—
mark me!—in life my spirit never roved beyond the
narrow limits of our money-changing hole; and weary
journeys lie before me!" . . .

"How it is that I appear before you in a shape that
you can see, I may not tell. I have sat invisible beside
you many and many a day."

It was not an agreeable idea. Scrooge shivered and wiped the perspiration from his brow.

The ghostly figure of Jacob Marley arrives in Scrooge's room in an unbearable clatter of chains and metal cash boxes, echoing throughout the house. And Marley—aside from the fact that Scrooge can see right through him—looks exactly like Scrooge remembers him before he died seven years ago.

This is not a happy reunion of old friends, however.

Ebenezer fights against all of his senses to deny that Jacob Marley is real. He tries reasoning Jacob's ghost away as a dream or hallucination caused by indigestion. *Ghosts aren't real, ghosts aren't real, ghosts aren't real,* his inner monologue plays on a loop.

But Marley has an important message for Scrooge, so he does what ghosts do best to scare Scrooge into listening to him. And it works. The normally stoic and indifferent Scrooge swoons and falls to his knees and begs for mercy. Finally, Jacob Marley is able to warn Ebenezer Scrooge that the heavy chains he wears and the fate he suffers by wandering the earth in agony will be Scrooge's fate, too—unless he changes his ways.

It may be that Scrooge is blissfully unaware that the path he has chosen—a miserly life of self-centeredness—is headed straight for destruction. But the consequences of this life are lengthening link by link in the chain he may someday be forced to carry with him through all eternity.

We often learn from our mistakes, but the wisest among

us will learn from the mistakes others make and avoid the same fate. With a visit from Jacob Marley, Scrooge is told exactly how his evil ways will play out if he does not change. We, like Scrooge, might think we have everything under control, but when there is sin in our lives, without repentance, sin will ultimately lead to destruction (Proverbs 14:12).

Jesus tells a similar story in Luke 16 of a rich man and Lazarus. The rich man lived a life of luxury with plenty to eat and drink and fine clothes to wear, while a homeless man named Lazarus, who was afflicted with sores, longed for leftover scraps from the rich man's table. The time came when Lazarus died and went to heaven where Abraham was, and the rich man died and went to hell, but he could still see Lazarus and Abraham in the distance. In Jesus' words:

> "The rich man shouted, 'Father Abraham, have some pity! Send Lazarus over here to dip the tip of his finger in water and cool my tongue. I am in anguish in these flames.'
>
> "But Abraham said to him, 'Son, remember that during your lifetime you had everything you wanted, and Lazarus had nothing. So now he is here being comforted, and you are in anguish. And besides, there is a great chasm separating us. No one can cross over to you from here, and no one can cross over to us from there.'
>
> "Then the rich man said, 'Please, Father Abraham, at least send him to my father's home. For I have five brothers, and I want him to warn them so they don't end up in this place of torment.'
>
> "But Abraham said, 'Moses and the prophets have

warned them. Your brothers can read what they wrote.'

"The rich man replied, 'No, Father Abraham! But if someone is sent to them from the dead, then they will repent of their sins and turn to God.'

"But Abraham said, 'If they won't listen to Moses and the prophets, they won't be persuaded even if someone rises from the dead.' " (verses 24–31 NLT)

God can work in any situation, no matter how dire—even if that means we learn from the mistakes that others make. Think of it: God loves us so much that He sacrificed the life of His Son. He will go to beyond the ends of the earth to save us. He is mighty and His love is mighty!

For God so loved the world that he gave his one and only Son, that whoever believes in him shall not perish but have eternal life.
JOHN 3:16 NIV

SCROOGE TAKES HIS MEDICINE

"I am here tonight to warn you, that you have yet a chance and hope of escaping my fate. A chance and hope of my procuring, Ebenezer." . . .

"You will be haunted," resumed the Ghost, "by three Spirits."

Scrooge's countenance fell almost as low as the Ghost's had done.

"Is that the chance and hope you mentioned, Jacob?" he demanded in a faltering voice.

"It is."

"I—I think I'd rather not," said Scrooge.

"Without their visits," said the Ghost, "you cannot hope to shun the path I tread. Expect the first tomorrow, when the bell tolls one."

"Couldn't I take 'em all at once, and have it over, Jacob?" hinted Scrooge.

"Expect the second on the next night at the same hour. The third, upon the next night when the last stroke of twelve has ceased to vibrate. Look to see me no more; and look that, for your own sake, you remember what has passed between us!"

After an impressive display of haunting and moaning and clanging chains and convincing Scrooge that he is real, Jacob Marley is finally able to get to the point of his visit to his old business partner. Marley tells Scrooge he will be visited by three spirits as the clock strikes the wee hours of Christmas morning.

It's obvious Scrooge has already had his fill of other-worldly visitors when he asks to be excused from hosting the ghostly guests, but Marley is insistent. The only way Scrooge can hope to escape his same fate is to follow the rules.

So Scrooge tries another tactic: bargaining. "How about if all three ghosts come at once?" It's a sort of rip-off-the-Band-Aid approach.

Jacob Marley doesn't even acknowledge Ebenezer's suggestion. Scrooge doesn't have to like it, but he is going to take his medicine and face the consequences of his actions.

Have you ever had to take medicine that tastes downright terrible? Medicine so disgusting that you have to plug your nose and close your eyes and count to three before you can send it down the hatch? Why would anyone put themselves through such torture? Because when we are sick, we know that taking that wretched medicine will ultimately help us feel better and return to health.

We all make wrong decisions. Because we are imperfect people, not a day goes by that we don't look back at a situation or conversation and realize that we could have handled it better. But once in a while, we make a mistake that causes a ripple effect that could grow from ripple to wave proportions. Sooner or later we have to deal with the consequences of that mistake. We might see the consequence coming a mile away or it might come out of nowhere, but it's coming, and it's best to face it head-on.

The Bible uses the metaphor of a farmer to explain how consequences work in Galatians 6:

> *Don't be misled—you cannot mock the justice of God.*
> *You will always harvest what you plant. Those who*

live only to satisfy their own sinful nature will harvest decay and death from that sinful nature. But those who live to please the Spirit will harvest everlasting life from the Spirit. So let's not get tired of doing what is good. At just the right time we will reap a harvest of blessing if we don't give up. Therefore, whenever we have the opportunity, we should do good to everyone—especially to those in the family of faith. (verses 7–10 NLT)

Think of it this way: As we grow up, most of us require years of discipline and correction from our parents to learn right and wrong. Loving parents don't use discipline to be cruel. Even when discipline might be hard or even painful for their children, parents correct out of love for them. And so it is with God, the perfect loving Father who wants the best for us, His children.

"But consider the joy of those corrected by God! Do not despise the discipline of the Almighty when you sin. For though he wounds, he also bandages. He strikes, but his hands also heal."
JOB 5:17–18 NLT

MARLEY'S REGRET

The apparition walked backward from him; and at every step he took, the window raised itself a little, so that when the specter reached it, it was wide open. He beckoned Scrooge to approach, which he did. When they were within two paces of each other, Marley's Ghost held up his hand, warning him to come no nearer. Scrooge stopped.

Not so much in obedience, as in surprise and fear; for on the raising of the hand he became sensible of confused noises in the air; incoherent sounds of lamentation and regret; wailings inexpressibly sorrowful and self-accusatory. The specter, after listening for a moment, joined in the mournful dirge and floated out upon the bleak, dark night.

Scrooge followed to the window, desperate in his curiosity. He looked out.

The air was filled with phantoms, wandering hither and thither in restless haste, and moaning as they went. Every one of them wore chains like Marley's Ghost; some few (they might be guilty governments) were linked together; none were free. Many had been personally known to Scrooge in their lives. He had been quite familiar with one old ghost, in a white waistcoat, with a monstrous iron safe attached to his ankle, who cried piteously at being unable to assist a wretched woman with an infant, whom he saw below, upon a doorstep. The misery with them all was, clearly, that they sought to interfere, for good, in human matters, and had lost the power forever.

Whether these creatures faded into mist, or mist

enshrouded them, he could not tell. But they and their spirit voices faded together; and the night became as it had been when he walked home.

Scrooge closed the window and examined the door by which the Ghost had entered. It was double-locked, as he had locked it with his own hands, and the bolts were undisturbed. He tried to say "Humbug!" but stopped at the first syllable.

Jacob Marley could have exited Scrooge's bedchamber quietly through the double-locked door, leaving his old business partner with his thoughts. But even though Scrooge has already professed his belief that Marley is real, the Ghost is certain that once he leaves, Scrooge will convince himself it was all a dream. If this night is to have any impact on Scrooge's eternity, Marley needs to pull out all the stops.

A ghoulish wail rises from outside the bedroom window that opens behind Marley—a clamor of noise filled with sadness and the regrets of hundreds of lifetimes. Scrooge has never heard anything like it, and he is drawn to the window as Marley floats out to join the crowd.

What Ebenezer sees is a sky full of ghostly figures—all shackled and in the same kind of misery as Jacob. The ghosts seem to be tormented by the fact that they can't help the needs of the living. Although each one is burdened with different types of chains and heavy safes and lock boxes, they all have one thing in common: they are not free.

Feelings of regret and guilt can either be helpful or extremely harmful in our lives. Short term, a heavy conscience and feeling sorry for doing something wrong can encourage us to correct our mistakes and ask for forgiveness quickly. Long term, regret and guilt can eat away at our minds and hearts, sending us into times of unbearable worry and anxiety.

In 2 Corinthians, Paul writes about an instance when he pointed out a sin within the church in a previous letter, and he knows that the letter caused them to feel guilty about what had happened. Even though he didn't want to cause members of the church family sorrow, he is glad for it because it led to their repentance. He explains the difference:

> *Godly sorrow brings repentance that leads to salvation and leaves no regret, but worldly sorrow brings death. (7:10 NIV)*

Regret left by itself to grow can lead to a life of chains and guilt and ultimate destruction. But regret followed quickly by repentance will result in a life of freedom and salvation in Christ Jesus for all of eternity. If your spirit is weighed down today by guilt, make the decision to choose freedom instead!

> *For you have been called to live in freedom, my brothers and sisters. But don't use your freedom to satisfy your sinful nature. Instead, use your freedom to serve one another in love.*
> GALATIANS 5:13 NLT

Stave Two

ANTICIPATION

Scrooge lay in this state until the chime had gone three quarters more, when he remembered, on a sudden, that the Ghost had warned him of a visitation when the bell tolled one. He resolved to lie awake until the hour was passed; and, considering that he could no more go to sleep than go to heaven, this was, perhaps, the wisest resolution in his power.

The quarter was so long, that he was more than once convinced he must have sunk into a doze unconsciously, and missed the clock. At length it broke upon his listening ear.

"Ding, dong!"

"A quarter past," said Scrooge, counting.

"Ding, dong!"

"Half past," said Scrooge.

"Ding, dong!"

"A quarter to it," said Scrooge.

"Ding, dong!"

"The hour itself," said Scrooge triumphantly, "and nothing else!"

He spoke before the hour bell sounded, which it now did with a deep, dull, hollow, melancholy ONE.

Although Ebenezer had mostly convinced himself that his visit from Jacob Marley was just a dream, he can't be completely sure until 1:00 a.m. comes and goes without any ghost visitors. Just fifteen more minutes and Scrooge can sleep peacefully for the rest of the night. But the next quarter hour is the longest of his life.

Anticipation is a fantastic emotion that we may experience more at Christmastime than other times of the year. Scrooge's anticipation is rooted in dread, but ours is rooted in joy!

What are you anticipating this year about Christmas? Maybe it's a long-standing family tradition like decorating the tree or making cookies or going caroling. Or maybe it's a gift that you're hoping to receive or give. Or a special trip or a visit from a family member you haven't seen in years. Christmas anticipation fills us with hope for the fun, love, and excitement that are wrapped up in our holiday experiences.

More than two thousand years ago, God's chosen people eagerly awaited the arrival of the Messiah. After all, God had promised to send His Son, and He could arrive anytime. Even though they didn't know exactly who or what to expect, they certainly looked forward to it!

But waiting is the hardest part. For children waiting for Christmas morning, Christmas Eve is the longest night of the year—the night when it's most difficult to fall asleep. The Jewish people had been waiting for much longer than that. For generations they held on to the promise of a King who would save them.

Finally, the night of the Messiah's coming arrived. Born to a Jewish teenager in a cave where farm animals slept, Jesus entered the world as a tiny baby in humble circumstances. God sent an angel to make the very first birth announcement to a group of shepherds. The Savior is here!

"Don't be afraid!" he said. "I bring you good news that will bring great joy to all people. The Savior—yes, the Messiah, the Lord—has been born today in Bethlehem, the city of David! And you will recognize him by this sign: You will find a baby wrapped snugly in strips of cloth, lying in a manger." (Luke 2:10–12 NLT)

As believers, today we await Jesus' return to earth when He will take us to heaven to live forever with God. Scripture tells us that only God knows when this will happen (Matthew 24:36). Think of it! We are waiting for this wonderful day with the same kind of anticipation as Jesus— and we can live in this joyous state of waiting every day! One thing we do know about His return is that it will be exciting and triumphant—much different than His birth in a stable. Here is how Jesus describes His return to earth in Luke 21:

"Then everyone will see the Son of Man coming on a cloud with power and great glory. So when all these things begin to happen, stand and look up, for your salvation is near!" (verses 27–28 NLT)

Celebrate this season of Christmas anticipation by living a life of anticipation of the wonderful plans God has for you!

I wait for the Lord. My soul waits and I hope in His Word. My soul waits for the Lord more than one who watches for the morning; yes, more than one who watches for the morning.
PSALM 130:5–6 NLV

THE GHOST OF CHRISTMAS PAST

It was a strange figure—like a child; yet not so like a child as like an old man, viewed through some supernatural medium, which gave it the appearance of having receded from the view, and being diminished to a child's proportions. Its hair, which hung about its neck and down its back, was white, as if with age; and yet the face had not a wrinkle in it, and the tenderest bloom was on the skin. The arms were very long and muscular; the hands the same, as if its hold were of uncommon strength. Its legs and feet, most delicately formed, were, like those upper members, bare. It wore a tunic of the purest white; and round its waist was bound a lustrous belt, the sheen of which was beautiful. It held a branch of fresh, green holly in its hand; and, in singular contradiction to that wintry emblem, had its dress trimmed with summer flowers. But the strangest thing about it was that from the crown of its head there sprung a bright, clear jet of light, by which all this was visible; and which was doubtless the occasion of its using, in its duller moments, a great extinguisher for a cap, which it now held under its arm.

Even this, though, when Scrooge looked at it with increasing steadiness, was not its strangest quality. For as its belt sparkled and glittered now in one part and now in another, and what was light one instant at another time was dark, so the figure itself fluctuated in its distinctness: being now a thing with one arm, now with one leg, now with twenty legs, now a pair of legs without a head, now a head without a body; of which dissolving parts no outline would be visible in the dense gloom wherein they melted away. And, in the very wonder of this, it would be itself again, distinct and clear as ever.

The first Ghost arrives precisely at the stroke of one, in a blinding burst of light that cuts through the darkness and shocks Scrooge's senses. Although Jacob Marley's ghost was disturbing, at least that one looked and sounded human. This Ghost—the Ghost of Christmas Past—well, this one is beyond anything Scrooge's pitiful imagination could have come up with.

Even with all the strange, indescribable characteristics of this Ghost, there is one thing that Scrooge can clearly see: a bright, clear jet of light shoots out of the Ghost's head. Scrooge squints at the light as he tries to take in this bizarre creature standing in front of him. Child or old man? White hair and tunic? Holly branch and summer flowers? Does that hat under the Ghost's arm look like a candle extinguisher? Scrooge rubs his eyes as parts of the Ghost seem to appear and disappear from his sight. The dreams are becoming even more ridiculous!

Have you ever felt strange or out of place because of your faith in God? Maybe someone has called you out for being different or for holding different beliefs or values than them. Maybe you have chosen to wear different clothes or listen to different music or read different books than the rest of the world, and your friends or family just don't understand why you do what you do.

Jesus tells us in John 15 that it's good if other people

aren't sure what to make of us or even don't like us, just like they weren't sure what to make of Him while He lived on earth:

> *"If you belonged to the world, the world would love you as its own. You do not belong to the world. I have chosen you out of the world and the world hates you." (verse 19 NLV)*

Jesus goes on to say that even though we live in the world, this world isn't our home—just like it wasn't Jesus' home. But we live here now to share His loving truth with a world that doesn't know it (John 17:15–18).

It's easy to go along with what the rest of the world is doing, thinking, and saying. But God calls us to a higher heavenly calling in our actions, thoughts, and words. We aren't here on earth to be strange just because. We're here to be different in a way that causes other people to want to see what we're all about!

> *If then you have been raised with Christ,*
> *keep looking for the good things of heaven. This is*
> *where Christ is seated on the right side of God.*
> *Keep your minds thinking about things in heaven.*
> *Do not think about things on the earth.*
> COLOSSIANS 3:1–2 NLV

LIGHT SNUFFERS

"Are you the Spirit, sir, whose coming was foretold to me?" asked Scrooge.

"I am!"

The voice was soft and gentle. Singularly low, as if instead of being so close beside him, it were at a distance.

"Who and what are you?" Scrooge demanded.

"I am the Ghost of Christmas Past."

"Long past?" inquired Scrooge, observant of its dwarfish stature.

"No. Your past."

Perhaps Scrooge could not have told anybody why, if anybody could have asked him, but he had a special desire to see the Spirit in his cap, and begged him to be covered.

"What!" exclaimed the Ghost, "would you so soon put out, with worldly hands, the light I give? It is not enough that you are one of those whose passions made this cap, and force me through whole trains of years to wear it low upon my brow?" Scrooge reverently disclaimed all intention to offend or any knowledge of having wilfully "bonneted" the Spirit at any period of his life. He then made bold to inquire what business brought him there.

"Your welfare!" said the Ghost.

---

nce Ebenezer recovers from his initial shock of the Ghost's appearance, he finds the words to ask some questions. Scrooge finds out that this is, indeed, the ghost he has been waiting for—the Ghost of Christmas Past.

"Christmases throughout history?" Scrooge asks, wondering if he might get to see the birth of the Christ child.

"No. Christmases of your personal history," the Ghost explains.

Scrooge hasn't thought about any Christmas from his past—ever. Since he chooses to neither celebrate nor acknowledge the day presently, he sees no reason to reminisce about years long forgotten.

The old man squints uncomfortably as he tries to look into the brightly lit face of the Ghost, hoping to see whether it is friend or foe. As the light beaming from the Ghost's head sears into Scrooge's eyes, he feels an almost uncontrollable urge to snuff out the light like a candle flame with the hat under the Ghost's arm.

Scrooge surrounds himself with darkness every day. As miserly as he is, he skimps on fires and candles—allowing just enough light and heat as necessary. When Scrooge is confronted with the pure light coming from the Ghost, unsurprisingly, his immediate reaction is to want to turn it off.

We all know people like this. They're light snuffers who find the bad in every situation. They live in misery, and whether they mean to or not, they bring a dark cloud with them wherever they go. They may even prefer being in the dark to being in the light.

For much of his life, Ebenezer Scrooge has allowed darkness to rule his heart, both by living in literal darkness and by building a wall between himself and others. Throughout history humans have associated darkness with things like dishonesty, corruption, and crime, and scripture describes evil and Satan as darkness (Ephesians 6:12).

The good news is that God has made a way for light to enter the world and conquer the darkness—through His Son and us, His children. Jesus describes Himself in scripture as the "light of the world" (John 8:12), and He promises that when we follow Him, that light will illuminate our paths. But even better than that, we can shine a light all around us—a "bright, clear jet of light" just like the Ghost of Christmas Present. Here is how Jesus put it as he spoke to a group of His followers in Matthew 5:

> *"You are the light of the world. You cannot hide a city that is on a mountain. Men do not light a lamp and put it under a basket. They put it on a table so it gives light to all in the house. Let your light shine in front of men. Then they will see the good things you do and will honor your Father Who is in heaven." (verses 14–16 NLV)*

Christmas, especially, is a time for shining light in the world. It's a time for blessing others in the name of Jesus. It's a time to make someone's day a little brighter through our words and actions. It's a perfect time to share the hope we have in Jesus with people who do not know Him. Everything is a little brighter at Christmas, and we can be a brighter light, too!

> *If we live in the light as He is in the light, we share what we have in God with each other. And the blood of Jesus Christ, His Son, makes our lives clean from all sin.*
> 1 JOHN 1:7 NLV

TRYING NEW THINGS

It put out its strong hand as it spoke, and clasped him gently by the arm.

"Rise, and walk with me!"

It would have been in vain for Scrooge to plead that the weather and the hour were not adapted to pedestrian purposes; that his bed was warm, and the thermometer a long way below freezing; that he was clad but lightly in his slippers, dressing gown, and nightcap; and that he had a cold upon him at that time. The grasp, though gentle as a woman's hand, was not to be resisted. He rose; but finding that the Spirit made toward the window, clasped its robe in supplication.

"I am a mortal," Scrooge remonstrated, "and liable to fall."

"Bear but a touch of my hand there," said the Spirit, laying it upon his heart, "and you shall be upheld in more than this!"

As the words were spoken, they passed through the wall, and stood upon an open country road, with fields on either hand. The city had entirely vanished. Not a vestige of it was to be seen. The darkness and the mist had vanished with it, for it was a clear, cold, winter day, with snow upon the ground.

From the time Scrooge left the office of Scrooge & Marley several hours earlier, all he really wanted was to be left alone for a deep winter's slumber in the only place in his house that was warm—his bed. That plan has failed miserably as he has now had two visitors in his bedroom, with the promise of two more before the night is over. And for a man who has never entertained in his home, Scrooge doesn't know the first thing about hospitality, nor does he care.

As the Ghost of Christmas Past invites Scrooge to take a walk with him, Scrooge knows he doesn't really have a choice. So although he considers trying to talk the Ghost out of the trip to wherever they're going, he decides to hold his tongue. . .until he sees the Ghost move toward the bedroom's second-story window. Scrooge may be a man of many talents, but flying is not one of them.

Everyone has Christmas traditions they look forward to every year. Some traditions span generations or entire churches or towns. These traditions are important, and they give us a sense of community and a foundation for belonging. But sometimes these traditions become so important to us that we become blind to other, better opportunities that God puts in our paths.

For example, imagine that a church has a long tradition of giving Christmas stockings filled with toys and candy to the children in the congregation. The church has done this for more than forty years, and multiple generations of children have looked forward to receiving their stockings every year. There is nothing wrong or sinful about this tradition, and every year it brings joy to families, even though the children open up presents at home as well.

Now imagine that the church hears about a need for presents for young residents at a local homeless shelter. If they can't do both and are unwilling to let go of their own tradition to help those in need, that's when it can become a barrier to doing good.

Paul explains it this way in 1 Corinthians:

We are allowed to do anything, but not everything is good for us to do. We are allowed to do anything, but not all things help us grow strong as Christians. Do not work only for your own good. Think of what you can do for others. (10:23–24 NLV)

What about you and your family? Do you allow room in your traditions and in your schedule to be unexpectedly used for good? It's easy to get complacent in our daily routines and errand lists. If you find yourself saying things like "It's what we always do" or "We have to," examine your motives and really think about and talk about why you're doing what you're doing.

Opportunities for giving and blessing others are all around us. Step out of your comfort zone and try something out of the ordinary. If you are seeking good and God's will, He will bless your traditions—both new and old.

Trust in the LORD with all your heart; do not depend on your own understanding. Seek his will in all you do, and he will show you which path to take.
PROVERBS 3:5–6 NLT

A THOUSAND ODORS
FLOATING IN THE AIR

As the words were spoken, they passed through the wall, and stood upon an open country road, with fields on either hand. The city had entirely vanished. Not a vestige of it was to be seen. The darkness and the mist had vanished with it, for it was a clear, cold, winter day, with snow upon the ground.

"Good heaven!" said Scrooge, clasping his hands together, as he looked about him. "I was bred in this place. I was a boy here!"

The Spirit gazed upon him mildly. Its gentle touch, though it had been light and instantaneous, appeared still present to the old man's sense of feeling. He was conscious of a thousand odors floating in the air, each one connected with a thousand thoughts and hopes and joys and cares long, long forgotten!

"Your lip is trembling," said the Ghost. "And what is that upon your cheek?"

Scrooge muttered, with an unusual catching in his voice, that it was a pimple, and begged the Ghost to lead him where he would.

"You recollect the way?" inquired the Spirit.

"Remember it!" cried Scrooge with fervor, "I could walk it blindfold."

The Ghost and Scrooge fly through time and space, leaving London and fog behind, and arrive on a rural road in the English countryside on a clear winter's day.

Freshly fallen snow blankets the fields on either side, and Ebenezer is surprised to recognize the area as the place where he lived as a boy.

Scrooge sniffs the air, catching the scent of the trees, the animals in the barn, and the wood smoke from the fireplace—and flashes of his childhood flood his mind. Fleeting feelings of hope and joy and living a carefree life flit through Scrooge's chest—feelings he hasn't experienced in decades. It seems so foreign to the old man, as if he is watching scenes from someone else's life. And although he can feel the memories slipping from his grasp, he tries in a desperate moment to hold on to them as long as he can.

"Are you crying? What is that on your cheek?" The Ghost's questions aren't accusing or mocking. No living soul had ever seen Scrooge show such tender emotion.

Yanked out of his memories by the Ghost's question, Scrooge quickly wipes his leaking eyes with his robe's sleeve and claims the thing on his cheek is a pimple. The Ghost smiles.

When the Ghost took Scrooge back to his childhood home, he experienced a phenomena called "olfactory memory." Certain odors may remind us of our past, and scientists think one reason for this is because the smell-analyzing region of our brain is closely connected to the regions that handle memory and emotion. The many smells of Christmas may bring back fond and vivid memories: a smell of pine brings back a trip to the Christmas tree farm, the smell of peppermint brings back a favorite candy that Grandma made.

Our five human senses (taste, touch, sight, hearing, and smell) by themselves are part of the complex creations that God so lovingly crafted, but it's amazing to think that these senses work together in such a mysterious way to nearly transport us to another time and another place!

Scripture uses the metaphor of smell to describe how our lives should be a pleasant aroma as we share God's love with others:

Now he uses us to spread the knowledge of Christ everywhere, like a sweet perfume. Our lives are a Christ-like fragrance rising up to God. (2 Corinthians 2:14–15 NLT)

One way to think of this is that when we interact with others, we want our spirit to be memorable in the same way a pleasant scent is memorable. Here are some practical ways to share your beautiful scent with others:

- Treat them the way you would like to be treated.
- Go out of your way to make sure they know you appreciate them.
- Ask them about something they're involved in or interested in.
- Truly care about them.

But our aroma isn't reserved just for other people. When we follow God's commandments and make sacrifices to live in faith, our lives are a wonderful, pleasing aroma to Him as well. Imagine it, the delicious smell of our love for others reminds God of just how much He loves us, too! That's an olfactory memory for eternity!

Therefore, I urge you, brothers and sisters, in view of God's mercy, to offer your bodies as a living sacrifice, holy and pleasing to God—this is your true and proper worship.
ROMANS 12:1 NIV

"BUT IT'S TOO LATE NOW"

"The school is not quite deserted," said the Ghost. "A solitary child, neglected by his friends, is left there still."

Scrooge said he knew it. And he sobbed.

They left the highroad, by a well-remembered lane, and soon approached a mansion of dull red brick, with a little weathercock surmounted cupola on the roof, and a bell hanging in it. It was a large house, but one of broken fortunes; for the spacious offices were little used, their walls were damp and mossy, their windows broken, and their gates decayed. . . .

They went, the Ghost and Scrooge, across the hall to a door at the back of the house. It opened before them and disclosed a long, bare, melancholy room, made barer still by lines of plain deal forms and desks. At one of these, a lonely boy was reading near a feeble fire; and Scrooge sat down upon a form and wept to see his poor forgotten self as he had used to be.

Not a latent echo in the house, not a squeak and scuffle from the mice behind the paneling, not a drip from the half-thawed water spout in the dull yard behind, not a sigh among the leafless boughs of one despondent poplar, not the idle swinging of an empty storehouse door, no, not a clicking in the fire, but fell upon the heart of Scrooge with softening influence, and gave a freer passage to his tears. . . .

Then, with a rapidity of transition very foreign to his usual character, he said, in pity for his former self, "Poor boy!" and cried again. . . .

"I wish," Scrooge muttered, putting his hand in his pocket and looking about him, after drying his eyes with his cuff, *"but it's too late now."*

"What is the matter?" asked the Spirit.

"Nothing," said Scrooge, *"nothing. There was a boy singing a Christmas carol at my door last night. I should like to have given him something, that's all."*

As Scrooge and the Ghost meander through Ebenezer's old stomping grounds, the sights, sounds, and people they encounter are as familiar to Scrooge as if he had been a boy just yesterday. He feels a bit self-conscious about being seen in his robe until the Ghost explains that what they're seeing are just shadows of the past and no one is aware of their presence.

Soon the pair arrive at Scrooge's school, deserted for the Christmas holiday—except for one solitary boy named Ebenezer. Forgotten by his friends and family, he reads silently with only the characters in his adventure books for company. Old Scrooge weeps openly now, with no excuse or apology.

A sense of lonely solitude, of feeling worthless and forgettable, washes over Scrooge, and such pity wells in his heart for his younger self. Like a flash, a memory of the previous night flits across his mind: the lone caroler outside his office door singing "God Rest Ye Merry, Gentlemen" through chattering teeth with his small hand outstretched. Perhaps he, too, was forgotten at Christmas and had no one to spend time with. "I wish I would've given him something," Scrooge laments, wiping his face with his damp sleeve, "but it's too late now."

We all are guilty of procrastinating from time to time. Even the most organized and disciplined among us will come across a task or responsibility that we just don't want to do right now, so it waits till tomorrow. Procrastination, at its simplest level, just shifts our tasks to a later time, and if the task is time sensitive, it means we will be working under a deadline, which can be stressful and make the task even more difficult to finish. And then there is the kind of procrastination that makes us miss an opportunity we will never get again. This kind of procrastination can lead to regret that we didn't seize the moment to do the very best thing.

Our heavenly Father, in His unending love for us, gives us opportunities every day to do the best thing, to be kind to others, to fill a need, to show His love. But when we see those chances for good, it's important that we take them right then and there, before the opportunity passes by. Here are some wise words from Proverbs about that very thing:

> *Do not withhold good from those who deserve it when it's in your power to help them. If you can help your neighbor now, don't say, "Come back tomorrow, and then I'll help you." (3:27–28 NLT)*

Will you allow a little room in your schedule today to do the best thing when God puts the opportunity in your path? Promising yourself you will do it tomorrow will be tempting, but you never know what tomorrow will bring. It's not too late—for us or for Scrooge. So do it! Do it now and be blessed!

*So be careful how you live. Don't live like fools,
but like those who are wise. Make the most of every
opportunity in these evil days. Don't act thoughtlessly,
but understand what the Lord wants you to do.*

Ephesians 5:15–17 NLT

CHRISTMAS FORGIVENESS

Scrooge looked at the Ghost, and with a mournful shaking of his head, glanced anxiously toward the door.

It opened, and a little girl, much younger than the boy, came darting in, and, putting her arms about his neck and often kissing him, addressed him as her "dear, dear brother."

"I have come to bring you home, dear brother!" said the child, clapping her tiny hands and bending down to laugh. "To bring you home, home, home!"

"Home, little Fan?" returned the boy.

"Yes!" said the child, brimful of glee. "Home, for good and all. Home, for ever and ever. Father is so much kinder than he used to be, that home's like heaven! He spoke so gently to me one dear night when I was going to bed that I was not afraid to ask him once more if you might come home; and he said yes, you should; and sent me in a coach to bring you. And you're to be a man!" said the child, opening her eyes, "and are never to come back here; but first, we're to be together all the Christmas long and have the merriest time in all the world."

"You are quite a woman, little Fan!" exclaimed the boy.

She clapped her hands and laughed, and tried to touch his head; but, being too little, laughed again and stood on tiptoe to embrace him. Then she began to drag him, in her childish eagerness, toward the door; and he, nothing loath to go, accompanied her.

The years of Scrooge's lonely Christmases at school fast-forward in front of his eyes, but he feels the sting of each holiday as it speeds by. In a moment, the scene slows to show a particular Christmas that Scrooge had forgotten—the one when he got to go home.

Ebenezer and his father hadn't spoken in years. The senior Scrooge was a lover of sport and all things manly, and from the age of four when Ebenezer picked up his first book and fell in love with reading, father and son had nothing in common. Father tried his very best to mold young Ebenezer to be just like him, and it quickly drove a wedge between the two. And the boarding school gave the boy the perfect place to stay away from Father for the majority of the year—even Christmas.

But as Father grew older, he softened a bit. Even little Fan was bold enough to ask if her brother might be allowed to come for Christmas this year. The elder Scrooge would try harder to connect with Ebenezer. After all, he had but one son. . . .

Families are a blessing from God. In His loving wisdom, He created us to have connections with other people through shared lineage and DNA. The kinship we feel with people we are related to often results in the strongest and longest relationships we have in our lives. But families are made up of imperfect people with flaws and hang-ups and dysfunction and sin, so sometimes our blessed families can feel like a curse.

Within families, love is stronger but hurts can cut deeper. Stinging words can leave a lasting impression. Misunderstandings can fester and feelings can balloon to epic proportions. And then we have to see these people at Christmas!

Do you have any unresolved conflict in your family? Christmas is the best time to seek reconciliation and forgiveness; hearts are often softer, joy is keenly felt, and peace feels like it is within our grasp.

But forgiveness isn't something that is just a nice thing to do. God commands us to forgive:

Be kind and compassionate to one another, forgiving each other, just as in Christ God forgave you. (Ephesians 4:32 NIV)

Sometimes we think of forgiveness as something we're doing for the other person, but in reality, when we forgive, we're really freeing ourselves first. When we forgive someone who has done something wrong to us, we are no longer holding on to the grudge that weighs down our hearts. With God's help, we have the power to forgive others many times over, even if they haven't asked for forgiveness. How many times should we forgive? As many as it takes to live in freedom, according to Jesus:

Then Peter came to him and asked, "Lord, how often should I forgive someone who sins against me? Seven times?"
"No, not seven times," Jesus replied, "but seventy times seven!" (Matthew 18:21–22 NLT)

Whether you're the one who needs to forgive or the one who needs to ask for forgiveness, don't let this season pass by without making things right within your family.

Dear friends, let us continue to love one another, for love comes from God. Anyone who loves is a child of God and knows God.
1 JOHN 4:7 NLT

THE FEZZIWIGS

The Ghost stopped at a certain warehouse door and asked Scrooge if he knew it.

"Know it!" said Scrooge. "Was I apprenticed here?"

They went in. At sight of an old gentleman in a Welsh wig, sitting behind such a high desk that if he had been two inches taller he must have knocked his head against the ceiling, Scrooge cried in great excitement:

"Why, it's old Fezziwig! Bless his heart; it's Fezziwig alive again!"

Old Fezziwig laid down his pen and looked up at the clock, which pointed to the hour of seven. He rubbed his hands, adjusted his capacious waistcoat, laughed all over himself, from his shoes to his organ of benevolence and called out, in a comfortable, oily, rich, fat, jovial voice:

"Yo ho, there! Ebenezer! Dick!"

Scrooge's former self, now grown a young man, came briskly in, accompanied by his fellow apprentice.

"Dick Wilkins, to be sure!" said Scrooge to the Ghost. "Bless me, yes. There he is. He was very much attached to me, was Dick. Poor Dick! Dear, dear!"

"Yo ho, my boys!" said Fezziwig. "No more work tonight. Christmas Eve, Dick. Christmas, Ebenezer!"

The proprietor of the business, a man named Mr. Fezziwig, sits high at his desk wearing his signature wool cap, working away into the evening hours—something Scrooge always appreciated about his old boss. But Christmas Eve is no ordinary night, and as soon as the clock strikes seven, Fezziwig lays aside every thought of work for the sake of the annual company party. Mr. Fezziwig calls out to his new apprentices, Ebenezer and Dick, who come running—expecting their boss to give them an order to fill before calling it quits for the day.

But no! Tonight Fezziwig has an extra twinkle in his eye and a grin on his lips, and he cheerfully tells the boys there will be no more work this evening. Food and music and dancing and games and laughter lie in store!

The young Ebenezer is surprised by this display of childlike glee from his employer. Although Fezziwig has always been very genial and fair to his apprentices, he works hard and expects the same from his employees. Apparently Christmas is an exception. Fezziwig's excitement over the coming festivities is absolutely infectious, and the older Scrooge smiles at the memory of what is to come.

Scrooge looks back at his time learning from Fezziwig with fondness, and rightfully so. For a serious young man like Ebenezer who was so singularly focused, leisure time wasn't something he made time for. The young Scrooge may have even secretly thought that the annual party was nothing but a frivolous waste of funds, but still he saw the joy that such a party brought to everyone who attended (including himself).

Do you have a mentor like Mr. Fezziwig in your life? Mentors are individuals who have experience in whatever it is that you'd like to get better in. They are trusted advisers who can help guide you, answer questions, and challenge you to be better. Mentors are essential for things like growing in your chosen career or in your spiritual life. Mentors can be helpful in sports and fitness as well as weight loss and even things like volunteering and hobbies. Mentors have been there and done that, and they can help you reach your goals all the faster by pointing out the best way forward and setting an example to follow, just like Fezziwig displayed to his young apprentices.

The Bible encourages us to mentor others and seek out mentors for ourselves. There are people all around us that we can learn from, and in the church, it's especially true. Here is what 1 Peter 5 says:

> *To the elders among you, I appeal as a fellow elder and a witness of Christ's sufferings who also will share in the glory to be revealed: Be shepherds of God's flock that is under your care, watching over them—not because you must, but because you are willing, as God wants you to be; not pursuing dishonest gain, but eager to serve; not lording it over those entrusted to you, but being examples to the flock. And when the Chief Shepherd appears, you will receive the crown of glory that will never fade away.*
>
> *In the same way, you who are younger, submit yourselves to your elders. All of you, clothe yourselves with humility toward one another, because, "God opposes the proud but shows favor to the humble." (verses 1–5 NIV)*

God places special people in each of our lives—some we can learn from and others we can lead by example. Ask Him to open your eyes to new opportunities to do both.

Join together in following my example, brothers and sisters, and just as you have us as a model, keep your eyes on those who live as we do.
PHILIPPIANS 3:17 NIV

TRUE HOSPITALITY

"Hilli-ho!" cried old Fezziwig, skipping down from the high desk with wonderful agility. "Clear away, my lads, and let's have lots of room here! Hilli-ho, Dick! Chirrup, Ebenezer!"

Clear away! There was nothing they wouldn't have cleared away, or couldn't have cleared away, with old Fezziwig looking on. It was done in a minute. Every movable was packed off, as if it were dismissed from public life forevermore; the floor was swept and watered, the lamps were trimmed, fuel was heaped upon the fire; and the warehouse was as snug and warm and dry and bright a ballroom as you would desire to see upon a winter's night.

In came a fiddler with a music book, and went up to the lofty desk, and made an orchestra of it, and tuned like fifty stomachaches. In came Mrs. Fezziwig, one vast, substantial smile. In came the three Miss Fezziwigs, beaming and lovable. In came the six young followers whose hearts they broke. In came all the young men and women employed in the business. In came the housemaid, with her cousin, the baker. In came the cook, with her brother's particular friend, the milkman. In came the boy from over the way, who was suspected of not having board enough from his master, trying to hide himself behind the girl from next door but one, who was proved to have had her ears pulled by her mistress. In they all came, one after another; some shyly, some boldly, some gracefully, some awkwardly, some pushing, some pulling; in they all came, anyhow and everyhow. Away

*they all went, twenty couples at once; hands half round
and back again the other way; down the middle and up
again; round and round in various stages of affectionate
grouping; old top couple always turning up in the wrong
place; new top couple starting off again, as soon as they
got there; all top couples at last, and not a bottom one
to help them! When this result was brought about, old
Fezziwig, clapping his hands to stop the dance, cried
out, "Well done!"*

Most of the village has been talking about the Fezziwig
Christmas Eve party for weeks. Each year the guest
list seems to grow, and a rumor is going around that Mr. and
Mrs. Fezziwig don't plan to stop inviting more folks until the
warehouse is so full that the large sliding doors won't shut.

Fezziwig's young, able-bodied apprentices named
Ebenezer and Dick make quick work of clearing the
warehouse floor just minutes before it starts to fill with
flush-faced party guests. Young, old, tall, short, rotund, thin,
rich, and poor—all come wearing their Christmas finest
and carrying a dish or two to add to the table of holiday
delicacies. Children bedecked in paper crowns run circles in
the empty space as the fiddle player tunes his violin.

The music soon begins in full force and the crowd
dances—not well, but happily and with gusto. The robe-
wearing Scrooge stands with his hands clasped in front of
him, smiling at the recognition of the long-lost faces in the
crowd and tapping his foot to the tune of the jig. There are
so many guests—peers and employees of Mr. Fezziwig, but
also many folks whom Scrooge considered much beneath the

Fezziwigs. But on Christmas Eve with the Fezziwigs, the joy shared was among equals.

If you're like most people, the holiday season may mean your social calendar is a bit fuller than the rest of the year. From family reunions and company parties to white elephant gift exchanges, cookie swaps, and New Year's Eve celebrations, it's a time of togetherness with family and friends new and old.

Christmas, especially, is the perfect time to practice hospitality and invite others to spend time in our homes. Mr. and Mrs. Fezziwig knew the importance of hospitality, and they left an impression on Scrooge that he carried with him into old age.

Hospitality comes naturally to some people, while for others it's a challenge. But having people spend time under our roof is one of the best ways to build relationships, so God's Word gives us some guidance on how to do it well. First, the Bible tells us to be hospitable without grumbling (1 Peter 4:9 NIV). Second, we should show hospitality to strangers when a need arises. Hebrews 13:2 even says that when we do, sometimes we are taking care of angels without knowing it. And third, it's important to reach out to people who can't, for whatever reason, invite you back:

> "When you give a luncheon or dinner, do not invite
> your friends, your brothers or sisters, your relatives, or
> your rich neighbors; if you do, they may invite you back
> and so you will be repaid. But when you give a banquet,
> invite the poor, the crippled, the lame, the blind, and
> you will be blessed. Although they cannot repay you,
> you will be repaid at the resurrection of the righteous."
> (Luke 14:12–14 NIV)

Perhaps one reason God asks us to open our homes is because opening our houses also means opening our hearts. This Christmas ask God to show you who He wants you and your family to open your hearts to.

And do not forget to do good and to share with others, for with such sacrifices God is pleased.
Hebrews 13:16 niv

THE IMPORTANCE OF ENCOURAGEMENT

When the clock struck eleven, this domestic ball broke up. Mr. and Mrs. Fezziwig took their stations, one on either side of the door, and shaking hands with every person individually as he or she went out, wished him or her a merry Christmas. When everybody had retired but the two apprentices, they did the same to them; and thus the cheerful voices died away, and the lads were left to their beds, which were under a counter in the back shop.

During the whole of this time, Scrooge had acted like a man out of his wits. His heart and soul were in the scene, and with his former self. He corroborated everything, remembered everything, enjoyed everything, and underwent the strangest agitation. It was not until now, when the bright faces of his former self and Dick were turned from them, that he remembered the Ghost, and became conscious that it was looking full upon him, while the light upon its head burned very clear.

"A small matter," said the Ghost, "to make these silly folks so full of gratitude."

"Small!" echoed Scrooge.

The Spirit signed to him to listen to the two apprentices, who were pouring out their hearts in praise of Fezziwig, and, when he had done so, said: "Why! Is it not? He has spent but a few pounds of your mortal money: three or four, perhaps. Is that so much that he deserves this praise?"

"It isn't that," said Scrooge, heated by the remark, and speaking unconsciously like his former, not his latter self—"it isn't that, Spirit. He has the power to

render us happy or unhappy, to make our service light or burdensome, a pleasure or a toil. Say that his power lies in words and looks, in things so slight and insignificant that it is impossible to add and count 'em up; what then? The happiness he gives is quite as great as if it cost a fortune."

He felt the Spirit's glance, and stopped.

"What is the matter?" asked the Ghost.

"Nothing particular," said Scrooge.

"Something, I think?" the Ghost insisted.

"No," said Scrooge—"no. I should like to be able to say a word or two to my clerk just now. That's all."

As the party draws to a close, Mr. and Mrs. Fezziwig stand by the door to personally bid each guest good-bye. Men exchange hearty handshakes and slaps on the back with wide smiles and eyes that gleam in the cheery candlelight while rosy-cheeked women embrace with all the warmth of the holiday. Not a single moment of work was accomplished in the past four hours, but all agreed it was time well spent.

As the festivities fade away, Scrooge is snapped back to reality, where he is dressed in his robe and standing next to the Ghost of Christmas Past. Although the memories he is experiencing are just shadows of the past, they feel as real to him as the day they happened. And what a wonderful feeling he is left with!

Although Fezziwig expected hard work from his employees, he was also a kind man who was quick to encourage and add value to the people who worked for him.

Scrooge always felt accepted, appreciated, and important when he worked for Fezziwig. And then an image of Bob Cratchit flashes across Scrooge's mind. The old man is quite certain his clerk has never felt accepted, let alone appreciated or important while working at Scrooge & Marley.

Few things are as wonderful as receiving encouragement from others. It can lift our spirits, feed our souls, and spur us on to greater things. Encouragement can change a bad day to a great one and a sour attitude to a cheery one. We all need encouragers in our lives, and we need to be encouragers, too.

Encouraging others may seem like a scary or uncomfortable thing, but adding value to other people can come in many forms. It can be as simple as a smile and a sincere "How are you doing today?" to a coworker. It may be a little note of encouragement or offering to babysit for a young couple so they can go out for a date night. It may be spending time with an elderly relative or having coffee with a friend who needs a listening ear.

Encouragement starts in hearts that are thankful for God's love and care in our own lives. When we acknowledge how much He has done for us, encouraging others comes from an overflow in our hearts. Here is how the apostle Paul explained it in 2 Corinthians 1:

> *We give thanks to the God and Father of our Lord Jesus Christ. He is our Father Who shows us loving-kindness and our God Who gives us comfort. He gives us comfort in all our troubles. Then we can comfort other people who have the same troubles. We give the same kind of comfort God gives us. (verses 3–4 NLV)*

Through the Holy Spirit, we have the power to make a major difference in other people's lives. Encouragement doesn't have to cost a cent. It doesn't require specialized skills or expert knowledge. It means having a heart that is always open to others and then doing what we can to meet needs when we see them. It's a sure way to a joy-filled Christmas followed by 364 more days of joy.

Therefore encourage one another and build
each other up, just as in fact you are doing.
1 Thessalonians 5:11 niv

EBENEZER'S TWO MASTERS

For again Scrooge saw himself. He was older now, a man in the prime of life. His face had not the harsh and rigid lines of later years, but it had begun to wear the signs of care and avarice. There was an eager greedy, restless motion in the eye, which showed the passion that had taken root, and where the shadow of the growing tree would fall.

He was not alone, but sat by the side of a fair young girl in a mourning dress, in whose eyes there were tears, which sparkled in the light that shone out of the Ghost of Christmas Past.

"It matters little," she said softly. "To you, very little. Another idol has displaced me; and if it can cheer and comfort you in time to come, as I would have tried to do, I have no just cause to grieve."

"What idol has displaced you?" he rejoined.

"A golden one." . . .

"What then?" he retorted. "Even if I have grown so much wiser, what then? I am not changed toward you."

She shook her head.

"Am I?"

"Our contract is an old one. It was made when we were both poor, and content to be so, until, in good season, we could improve our worldly fortune by our patient industry. You are changed. When it was made, you were another man."

"I was a boy," he said impatiently.

"Your own feeling tells you that you were not what you are," she returned. "I am. That which promised

happiness when we were one in heart is fraught with misery now that we are two. How often and how keenly I have thought of this, I will not say. It is enough that I have thought of it, and can release you."

Years pass before Ebenezer's eyes until a certain scene comes into focus. Scrooge recognizes it immediately, and a rush of icy regret floods his stomach. The younger Ebenezer sits, no longer an apprentice but not yet an old man, next to a beautiful young woman named Belle. Ah, gentle, kind, and beautiful Belle. Scrooge never understood why she chose to love him. Awkward, bookish, workaholic Ebenezer felt dashing, charismatic, and important when he had such a lovely creature on his arm.

The couple entered their betrothal early in the relationship, with the hopes and dreams of a wonderful life together. Belle was eager to get married as soon as Ebenezer's apprenticeship was completed, but he wanted to establish his business first—to secure their future, he said. One year turned into two, two turned into five with gentle pleadings from the bride and more excuses from the groom. The business wasn't turning a profit yet. The prospects aren't quite where he would like them to be. Just a little more. More work. More time. More patience.

But today Belle finally realized she had lost the Ebbie that she had fallen for. The love she saw in his eyes was no longer for her; it was for money. So she let him go to pursue that love wholeheartedly.

Money touches our lives every day. Whether we're working to make it or spending it or saving it or borrowing it or wishing we had more of it, we all have to deal with it to live. Jesus knew the major role that money plays in our lives, and He spoke more about money in scripture than about heaven and hell combined. Nearly a third of Jesus' parables talk about money, and hundreds of scriptures deal with money in both the Old and New Testaments. Money is a big deal.

Money, in and of itself, is neither good nor bad, right nor wrong. Money is a powerful tool that can be used to promote goodness or evil. Scripture warns us that the biggest trap with money is when we develop a love for it:

> *The love of money is the beginning of all kinds of sin. Some people have turned from the faith because of their love for money. They have made much pain for themselves because of this. (1 Timothy 6:10 NLV)*

It may seem silly to think that we can fall in love with money. After all, it's not a living thing that can love us back, but money does provide us with a false sense of security. Money can cause us to feel invincible and to stop relying on God to provide our needs. Money can buy things we want and empower us to have influence over people and events. Having more and more money can make us feel really good. . .for a time. But just as Scrooge found out, love of money can lead to broken relationships (Proverbs 28:25). Jesus tells us that money can even ruin our most important relationship—our relationship with our heavenly Father:

> *"No one can serve two masters. Either you will hate the one and love the other, or you will be devoted to the one and despise the other. You cannot serve both God and money." (Matthew 6:24 NIV)*

In a battle between God's power and money's power, money doesn't stand a chance. Choose God's plan for money in your life, and above all, seek Him first.

Do not love the world or anything in the world.
If anyone loves the world, love for the Father is not
in them. For everything in the world—the lust of the flesh,
the lust of the eyes, and the pride of life—comes not from
the Father but from the world. The world and its desires
pass away, but whoever does the will of God lives forever.
1 John 2:15–17 niv

ENDING A RELATIONSHIP

"Have I ever sought release?"

"In words? No. Never."

"In what, then?"

"In a changed nature, in an altered spirit, in another atmosphere of life, another hope as its great end. In everything that made my love of any worth or value in your sight. If this had never been between us," said the girl, looking mildly, but with steadiness, upon him, "tell me, would you seek me out and try to win me now? Ah, no!"

He seemed to yield to the justice of this supposition, in spite of himself. But he said, with a struggle, "You think not."

"I would gladly think otherwise if I could," she answered. "Heaven knows! When I have learned a truth like this, I know how strong and irresistible it must be. But if you were free today, tomorrow, yesterday, can even I believe that you would choose a dowerless girl—you who, in your very confidence with her, weigh everything by gain; or, choosing her, if for a moment you were false enough to your own guiding principle to do so, do I not know that your repentance and regret would surely follow? I do, and I release you. With a full heart, for the love of him you once were."

He was about to speak, but, with her head turned from him, she resumed:

"You may—the memory of what is past half makes me hope you will—have pain in this. A very, very brief time, and you will dismiss the recollection of it, gladly, as an unprofitable dream, from which it happened well that you awoke. May you be happy in the life you have chosen!"

Ebenezer had always wondered if this day would come. Belle gives every good reason for why she is ending their long engagement, but despite the logic of all of it, he can nearly feel his heart being ripped from his chest. She has tried so long to see the good in him, but as the years go by, the good man she fell in love with has been replaced by a miserly workaholic whose one goal in life is *more*—more money, more power, more influence. All of Ebenezer's *more* has left Belle with *less*.

Belle doesn't want to hurt Ebenezer by letting him go, but between potentially breaking his heart or living a life with a man so coldhearted and unfeeling, she must take the chance and hope that his broken heart will heal. She has struggled with her decision for far too long. This relationship has taken a toll on her health and on her spirit, and she can bear it no longer. The relationship must end.

Sometimes relationships turn sour in such a way that they become toxic to our hearts and to our lives. Friendships and romantic relationships can slip into this dangerous category, and sometimes it happens so gradually that we are not even aware of it. Although our first goal should always be to reconcile and be at peace with others (Romans 12:18), sometimes the situation calls for a relationship to end—especially when we have done everything we can.

God's Word gives us guidance on the kind of people we should surround ourselves with and those we should avoid when we have the choice:

> *Walk with the wise and become wise; associate with fools and get in trouble. (Proverbs 13:20 NLT)*

Do not make friends with a hot-tempered person, do not associate with one easily angered, or you may learn their ways and get yourself ensnared. (Proverbs 22:24–25 NIV)

Can two people walk together without agreeing on the direction? (Amos 3:3 NLT)

How do you know when it's time to end a relationship? That's a difficult question and only one that you can answer for yourself and your situation. Pray and ask God for guidance in the relationship and for His healing, if it's His plan. Ask Him to work in the heart of the other person and to bless that person. Ask Him for the right words to say that will promote peace between you. And if it's time to end the relationship, ask Him to make that evident as well.

Every relationship goes through seasons of tough times, and usually we can come out on the other side with a stronger and better bond. When we focus on loving others, our relationships can and should be a blessing to us, to the other person, and to God.

Two people are better off than one, for they can help each other succeed. If one person falls, the other can reach out and help. But someone who falls alone is in real trouble. . . . Three are even better, for a triple-braided cord is not easily broken.
ECCLESIASTES 4:9–10, 12 NLT

93

CHILDLIKE WONDER

They were in another scene and place, a room, not very large or handsome, but full of comfort. Near to the winter fire sat a beautiful young girl, so like that last that Scrooge believed it was the same, until he saw her, now a comely matron, sitting opposite her daughter. The noise in this room was perfectly tumultuous, for there were more children there than Scrooge in his agitated state of mind could count; and, unlike the celebrated herd in the poem, they were not forty children conducting themselves like one, but every child was conducting itself like forty. The consequences were uproarious beyond belief; but no one seemed to care. . . .

But now a knocking at the door was heard, and such a rush immediately ensued that she, with laughing face and plundered dress, was borne toward it, in the center of a flushed and boisterous group, just in time to greet the father, who came home attended by a man laden with Christmas toys and presents. Then the shouting and the struggling, and the onslaught that was made on the defenseless porter! The scaling him, with chairs for ladders, to dive into his pockets, despoil him of brown-paper parcels, hold on tight by his cravat, hug him round the neck, pommel his back, and kick his legs in irrepressible affection! The shouts of wonder and delight with which the development of every package was received! The terrible announcement that the baby had been taken in the act of putting a doll's fryingpan into his mouth and was more than suspected of having swallowed a fictitious turkey, glued on a wooden platter!

The immense relief of finding this a false alarm! The joy, and gratitude, and ecstasy! They are all indescribable alike. It is enough that, by degrees, the children and their emotions got out of the parlor, and, by one stair at a time, up to the top of the house, where they went to bed, and so subsided.

A moment after old Scrooge witnesses the breakup of his engagement to Belle, the Ghost transports them to another Christmas scene. Scrooge realizes the setting is unfamiliar to him, but he recognizes the face of his beloved Belle, now a beautiful middle-aged woman, with a roomful of children, including an eldest daughter who looks so much like her mother that Scrooge does a double-take.

The energy of the younger children in the room is so intense that Scrooge can't keep track of all of them. How many are there? Forty? No, not nearly so many, but they certainly have the energy of forty children. And when their father arrives home, the excitement reaches an all-time high. Now Christmas Eve can really begin!

Father is accompanied by a deliveryman, whose arms are full of Christmas gifts. And when the children see him, their delight at the sight of the packages is too much to handle. The deliveryman doesn't know what hits him as the children fairly climb up his legs and arms and pick his pockets to find every surprise he has on his person. Mother and Father laugh despite themselves and peel the children off the disheveled deliveryman before Father gives him a generous tip, appropriate pay for the injustice he has just endured. It's Christmas, and the unbridled joy of children cannot be stopped.

Can you remember the wonder and delight you experienced as a child at Christmastime? December ushers in a time in a child's heart when lights are brighter, sweets are sweeter, surprises are joy-filled, magic is real, traditions are beloved foundations of family and home, and every day holds the potential of being the best day ever. Somewhere along the way as we age, lights dim, sweets go straight to our waistline, surprises require a lot of work, magic doesn't exist, traditions are a waste of time, and if we can just get through the holidays, life can go back to normal. Bah! Humbug!

We can learn much from the way children look at the world—both at Christmastime and in their faith journeys. Think about the time you first believed in Jesus. Maybe it was when you heard stories about His love for you or when you first felt the power of the Holy Spirit. Maybe it was the first time you prayed to God and felt His presence in your life. Did you feel excited, hopeful, joyful, safe, unafraid, or free to truly be the person He created you to be? All of the above? If you spend any time around children, you know that children tend to feel these emotions much more often than adults do.

Jesus knows that adults sometimes overlook children altogether. So when the disciples asked Jesus in Matthew 18 who would be the greatest in the kingdom of heaven, Jesus' response must have come as a surprise:

> *Jesus called a little child to him and put the child among them. Then he said, "I tell you the truth, unless you turn from your sins and become like little children, you will never get into the Kingdom of Heaven. So anyone who becomes as humble as this little child is the greatest in*

the Kingdom of Heaven. And anyone who welcomes
a little child like this on my behalf is welcoming me."
(verses 2–5 NLT)

In Matthew 21, we see the opposite reactions that
"religious" adults and children have when they are with Jesus:

The blind and the lame came to him in the Temple, and
[Jesus] healed them. The leading priests and the teachers
of religious law saw these wonderful miracles and heard
even the children in the Temple shouting, "Praise God
for the Son of David." But the leaders were indignant.
(verses 14–15 NLT)

"Pipe down out there!" we can almost hear the adult say.
But the children won't be silenced. In their childlike faith,
they see clearly what's most important—and it's a cause for
celebration!

If you're feeling more adultlike and less childlike this
Christmas, read the Christmas account in Luke 2 with
a child and experience the wonder and magic of God
becoming a human to live on earth with us. Joy is there for
the taking, so fill your heart and watch it overflow!

But Jesus said, "Let the children come to me. Don't stop
them! For the Kingdom of Heaven belongs to those who
are like these children." And he placed his hands on
their heads and blessed them before he left.
MATTHEW 19:14–15 NLT

WHAT COULD HAVE BEEN

And now Scrooge looked on more attentively than ever, when the master of the house, having his daughter leaning fondly on him, sat down with her and her mother at his own fireside; and when he thought that such another creature, quite as graceful and as full of promise, might have called him father, and been a springtime in the haggard winter of his life, his sight grew very dim indeed.

"Belle," said the husband, turning to his wife with a smile, "I saw an old friend of yours this afternoon."

"Who was it?"

"Guess!"

"How can I? Tut, don't I know?" she added in the same breath, laughing as he laughed. "Mr. Scrooge."

"Mr. Scrooge it was. I passed his office window; and as it was not shut up and he had a candle inside, I could scarcely help seeing him. His partner lies upon the point of death, I hear, and there he sat alone. Quite alone in the world, I do believe."

"Spirit!" said Scrooge, in a broken voice, "remove me from this place."

"I told you these were shadows of the things that have been," said the Ghost. "That they are what they are, do not blame me!"

"Remove me!" Scrooge exclaimed. "I cannot bear it!"

He turned upon the Ghost, and, seeing that it looked upon him with a face in which, in some strange way, there were fragments of all the faces it had shown him, wrestled with it.

As Belle's family settles in for a Christmas Eve together, Scrooge looks upon the scene and imagines what it would have been like if he were the father in this family. His life, such as it is, has passed in the blink of an eye, and although he had never regretted his loneliness (there had been far too much work to do and money to make to reflect on the what-could-have-beens), he now sees the life he could have had with Belle, if only. . . But the thought weighs on him, and he shoves it down deep just as Belle's husband begins to speak.

He saw Ebenezer Scrooge earlier that day, through the window at Scrooge & Marley, working away on Christmas Eve. It's no wonder, though. . .since he is doing the work of Jacob Marley as well, who is rumored to be gravely ill and likely to die anytime. Scrooge seemed so alone, Belle's husband said. The look of pity in Belle's eyes as she wiped away a stray tear rips something inside Scrooge's chest.

"Take me away from here!" Scrooge commands the Ghost of Christmas Past. But when he turns to look at the Ghost, Scrooge sees the faces of all the people who haunt his past, along with the mistakes he would like to take back and the Christmases he wishes he could do over.

Wouldn't it be nice if life had an UNDO button? Scrooge's list of undo wishes seems to be getting longer as the night passes. Hopefully your list isn't Scrooge-length, but we all have made decisions that led to consequences later on. Sometimes those consequences come quickly, but sometimes it can be days, months, or even years later when we realize our mistake.

We are imperfect people, and although as Christians we are saved by grace through Jesus Christ, we will still continue to be imperfect while we are here on earth. But God promises us that He is working on our hearts, and when we seek to be more like Him each day, we can look forward, rather than backward, with confidence:

"Forget the former things; do not dwell on the past. See, I am doing a new thing! Now it springs up; do you not perceive it? I am making a way in the wilderness and streams in the wasteland." (Isaiah 43:18–19 NIV)

Maybe, like Scrooge, you feel like your mistakes have you trapped in a wilderness, but God's living water is there! Seek it in prayer and in scripture meditation and in the conversations you have with friends who know God's love. Our heavenly Father is in the business of doing new things in our hearts and lives:

Anyone who belongs to Christ has become a new person. The old life is gone; a new life has begun! (2 Corinthians 5:17 NLT)

Do you have regrets from your past that you need to let go of so that God can fully do a new thing, set you on a new path, with His glorious plan ahead? God Himself promises never to think of our sins again once they are forgiven (Isaiah 43:25). Let go of the chains of yesterday and live in the joyful expectation of tomorrow!

My old self has been crucified with Christ. It is no longer I who live, but Christ lives in me. So I live in this earthly body by trusting in the Son of God, who loved me and gave himself for me.
GALATIANS 2:20 NLT

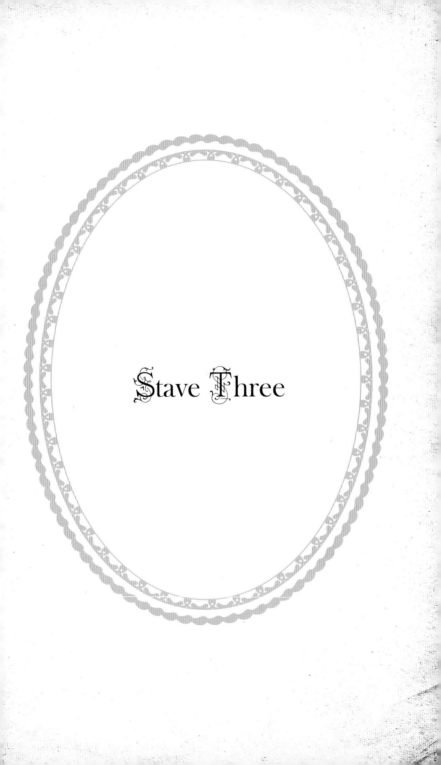

Stave Three

WHILE WE WAIT

*Without venturing for Scrooge quite as hardily as this,
I don't mind calling on you to believe that he was ready
for a good broad field of strange appearances, and that
nothing between a baby and a rhinoceros would have
astonished him very much.*

*Now, being prepared for almost anything, he
was not by any means prepared for nothing; and,
consequently, when the bell struck one, and no shape
appeared, he was taken with a violent fit of trembling.
Five minutes, ten minutes, a quarter of an hour went
by, yet nothing came. All this time he lay upon his bed,
the very core and center of a blaze of ruddy light, which
streamed upon it when the clock proclaimed the hour;
and which, being only light, was more alarming than
a dozen ghosts, as he was powerless to make out what it
meant, or would be at and was sometimes apprehensive
that he might be at that very moment an interesting
case of spontaneous combustion, without having the
consolation of knowing it. At last, however, he began
to think—as you or I would have thought at first; for
it is always the person not in the predicament who
knows what ought to have been done in it, and would
unquestionably have done it too—at last, I say, he
began to think that the source and secret of this ghostly
light might be in the adjoining room, from whence, on
further tracing it, it seemed to shine. This idea taking
full possession of his mind, he got up softly, and shuffled
in his slippers to the door.*

Scrooge awakens in his own bed just before the clock strikes one. At this point, he has little doubt that the next Ghost will arrive at any moment, and he is ready for anything. After all, Jacob promised visits from three ghosts, and the first was more astounding than Scrooge could have imagined himself. The clock strikes the hour, and Scrooge is thankful there is no other soul there to see the violent trembling that overtakes his body. Any moment now, the Ghost will appear. . .but the seconds turn to minutes, and the only sound Ebenezer hears is his own breathing and the ticking wall clock. Five minutes, now ten, now fifteen. The anticipation is worse than the actual arrival of the Ghost.

As he remains on alert, suddenly he is aware that he can see shapes in the blackness of his bedchamber. Could that ghostly light coming from beneath the bedroom door be what leads him to his next visitor?

Waiting isn't much fun. Living in the twenty-first century has many wonderful blessings, but our instant-gratification world sometimes makes our patience as short as our attention spans. Whether we are waiting in line at the store or in the exam room at the doctor's office, we tend to get antsy and impatient and even irritated and frustrated.

When we are part of God's family, He promises to hear our prayers (1 John 5:14–15), and He is faithful to answer us—but sometimes His answer for now is "Wait."

Waiting is always difficult, but we need to realize that God's time is different than ours. Although He gives us the knowledge to measure time in seconds, minutes, hours, days, and years, God doesn't wear a watch. He always *has been* and always *will be*, and He knows the exact time stamp for your prayer to be answered to fulfill His will.

Scripture records more than eight thousand prophetic verses that promise many things like the coming of Jesus, His death and resurrection, His second coming, and our eternity in heaven. Many of these verses have already been fulfilled, and some are yet to be fulfilled, but God is faithful and will make all of those promises come true, including the requests that we have made to Him. In His time.

While we wait, God promises to strengthen us through His Spirit:

But they who wait upon the Lord will get new strength. They will rise up with wings like eagles. They will run and not get tired. They will walk and not become weak. (Isaiah 40:31 NLV)

We wait in hope for the LORD; he is our help and our shield. In him our hearts rejoice, for we trust in his holy name. May your unfailing love be with us, LORD, even as we put our hope in you. (Psalm 33:20–22 NIV)

What answer to prayer are you awaiting this Christmas? Even while you wait, focus on the hope of this season. God's people had been asking for a Savior for generations, and God answered by sending the Messiah, the holy baby Jesus, on that peaceful night in Bethlehem so many years ago. He is faithful!

Trust in the LORD with all your heart; do not depend on your own understanding. Seek his will in all you do, and he will show you which path to take.
PROVERBS 3:5–6 NLT

THE GHOST OF CHRISTMAS PRESENT

In easy state upon this couch there sat a jolly Giant, glorious to see who bore a glowing torch, in shape not unlike Plenty's horn, and held it up, high up, to shed its light on Scrooge as he came peeping round the door.

"Come in!" exclaimed the Ghost—"come in and know me better, man!"

Scrooge entered timidly and hung his head before this Spirit. He was not the dogged Scrooge he had been and though the Spirit's eyes were clear and kind, he did not like to meet them.

"I am the Ghost of Christmas Present," said the Spirit. "Look upon me!"

Scrooge reverently did so. He was clothed in one simple, deep-green robe, or mantle, bordered with white fur. This garment hung so loosely on the figure that his capacious breast was bare, as if disdaining to be warded or concealed by any artifice. His feet, observable beneath the ample folds of the garment, were also bare, and on his head he wore no other covering than a holly wreath, set here and there with shining icicles. His dark-brown curls were long and free, free as his genial face, his sparkling eye, his open hand, his cheery voice, his unconstrained demeanor, and his joyful air. . . .

"You have never seen the like of me before!" exclaimed the Spirit.

"Never," Scrooge made answer to it.

Scrooge timidly opens the door from his bedroom into the glowing light from the torch of the Ghost of

Christmas Present. The old man blinks, not believing the decadent transformation of the room—from the roaring fire in the hearth, holly and glistening berries, mistletoe and ivy, to the roasted meats, plum puddings, ripe fruits, and every other Christmas delicacy imaginable. But most impressive of all is the giant Spirit sitting on a throne in the middle of the room.

The large, amiable man smiles broadly and invites the miserable old bird of a man in. Scrooge enters but doesn't look up—choosing instead to inspect his own slippers. The old man's odd demeanor makes the Ghost chuckle, and he introduces himself and tells Scrooge to look at him.

Scrooge isn't sure what to make of the look of this Ghost: a large, bare-chested and barefoot man dressed in a green robe with a holly wreath on his head with icicles hanging from it. In his hand he carries a torch in the shape of a cornucopia, which glows with a ghostly light. His hair flows from under his crown in long, dark curls, and his eyes sparkle like flickering candlelight. Scrooge thinks this giant Spirit is the strangest "man" he has ever seen. But he is not going to tell the Ghost that.

When we first meet someone face-to-face, our very first impressions may be based on the person's clothes, beauty (or lack thereof), or some other physical feature. Once we get to know someone through conversation and spending time together, hopefully any incorrect snap judgments we may inadvertently make will be set right.

From fashion magazines and Hollywood to reality TV and celebrity culture, this world wants us to believe that what we look like equals our worth, but that's the exact opposite of what God's Word tells us. When God sent the

Old Testament prophet Samuel to find the next king of Israel, he was distracted by Jesse's strong, handsome sons— any of whom would have looked fantastic in a crown. But God told Samuel to choose Jesse's young, inexperienced, unimpressive shepherd boy son named David:

> *But the Lord said to Samuel, "Do not look at the way he looks on the outside or how tall he is, because I have not chosen him. For the Lord does not look at the things man looks at. A man looks at the outside of a person, but the Lord looks at the heart." (1 Samuel 16:7 NLV)*

True beauty to our Father isn't found in the things the world says are attractive. Just as the joy of life radiated from the Ghost of Christmas Present, our lives can reflect the beautiful love of God. When we reflect that love to others, we reflect an inner beauty that is lovely to everyone around us. A cheerful heart (Proverbs 17:22), a peaceful spirit that shares God's good news (Isaiah 52:7), a pure heart and clear conscience and genuine faith (1 Timothy 1:5)—all of these are beautiful to God.

> *Don't be concerned about the outward beauty of fancy hairstyles, expensive jewelry, or beautiful clothes. You should clothe yourselves instead with the beauty that comes from within, the unfading beauty of a gentle and quiet spirit, which is so precious to God.*
> 1 PETER 3:3–4 NLT

IMPERFECT CHRISTMAS

Holly, mistletoe, red berries, ivy, turkeys, geese, game, poultry, brawn, meat, pigs, sausages, oysters, pies, puddings, fruit, and punch, all vanished instantly. So did the room, the fire, the ruddy glow, the hour of the night, and they stood in the city streets on Christmas morning, where (for the weather was severe) the people made a rough, but brisk and not unpleasant kind of music in scraping the snow from the pavement in front of their dwellings and from the tops of their houses, whence it was mad delight to the boys to see it come plumping down into the road below, and splitting into artificial little snowstorms.

The house fronts looked black enough, and the windows blacker, contrasting with the smooth white sheet of snow upon the roofs, and with the dirtier snow upon the ground; which last deposit had been plowed up in deep furrows by the heavy wheels of carts and wagons, furrows that crossed and recrossed each other hundreds of times where the great streets branched off, and made intricate channels, hard to trace in the thick yellow mud and icy water. The sky was gloomy, and the shortest streets were choked up with a dingy mist, half thawed, half frozen, whose heavier particles descended in a shower of sooty atoms, as if all the chimneys in Great Britain had, by one consent, caught fire, and were blazing away to their dear hearts' content. There was nothing very cheerful in the climate or the town, and yet there was an air of cheerfulness abroad that the clearest summer air and brightest summer sun might have endeavored to diffuse in vain.

For the people who were shoveling away on the housetops were jovial and full of glee, calling out to one another from the parapets, and now and then exchanging a facetious snowball—better-natured missile far than many a wordy jest—laughing heartily if it went right, and not less heartily if it went wrong.

The Ghost of Christmas Present wastes no time before ushering Scrooge outside to a typical London street, where the weather is less than ideal. Yes, it snowed overnight, but the beauty of the untouched blanket of white is long gone now, replaced with deep pathways and crevasses where shovels and brooms have uncovered the city's soot, grime, and muddy water underneath. The ever-present fog hangs in the air, not willing to give Londoners a clear sky even on Christmas morning. Despite all this, the joyous spirit of Christmas survives, and men, women, and children make games of the snow removal, and laughter fills the streets like the melody of a beloved holiday carol.

Do you long for the perfect Christmas? From magazines and blogs to jewelry store commercials and Food Network specials, there are a million voices shouting the five simple tips to a perfect family Christmas. Like a Norman Rockwell painting, we envision tasteful yet whimsical decorations, a delectable feast, festively dressed and behaved family members, and angelic children who are patient when opening presents and show no other emotion than pure ecstasy at every surprise they unwrap. And of course, the holy reading of the biblical account of Jesus' birth—where all in attendance are enraptured by the eternal significance of the story and take each word to heart with joyful gratitude.

Even with the best of intentions, our Christmas may end up looking more like a soot-filled London street than a freshly snow-blanketed country estate. Christmastime is often so filled with expectations that it's no wonder we find ourselves disappointed. There is nothing wrong with making plans, although it's important to realize that we don't have control—even at Christmas—but that doesn't mean the season can't be the most joyous time of year!

Just like the people in London, make the most of the bad weather in your holiday. Does the fifty-degree Christmas day shatter your expectation for a white Christmas? Take your family to the park, complete with a Christmas cookie picnic, and enjoy the nice weather. Does the bumper-to-bumper holiday traffic raise your blood pressure? Take a breath and admire the beauty of the Christmas lights that you'd normally be speeding by. Are the children uncooperative for the Christmas photo? Take the picture anyway and look forward to the years of laughs the family will get at the ridiculous faces they're making.

When we're obsessed with perfection—Christmas or otherwise—we're guaranteed to face disappointment. The Bible tells us that perfection can only be found in Jesus Christ:

> Let us keep looking to Jesus. Our faith comes from Him and He is the One Who makes it perfect. He did not give up when He had to suffer shame and die on a cross. He knew of the joy that would be His later. Now He is sitting at the right side of God. (Hebrews 12:2 NLV)

This Christmas choose to focus on joy rather than perfection. You won't be disappointed.

When my worry is great within me,
Your comfort brings joy to my soul.
PSALM 94:19 NLV

PEACEFUL CHRISTMAS

The sight of these poor revelers appeared to interest the Spirit very much, for he stood, with Scrooge beside him, in a baker's doorway, and, taking off the covers as their bearers passed, sprinkled incense on their dinners from his torch. And it was a very uncommon kind of torch, for once or twice when there were angry words between some dinner-carriers who had jostled each other, he shed a few drops of water on them from it, and their good humor was restored directly. For they said, it was a shame to quarrel upon Christmas Day. And so it was! God love it, so it was! . . .

It was a remarkable quality of the Ghost (which Scrooge had observed at the baker's), that notwithstanding his gigantic size, he could accommodate himself to any place with ease; and that he stood beneath a low roof quite as gracefully and like a supernatural creature as it was possible he could have done in any lofty hall.

While the rich of London are wearing their finery at Christmas morning church services, the poor fill the streets around Ebenezer and the Ghost. Many of these people don't have cookstoves at home, so they are taking their meager Christmas meals to the bakery. There the baker allows them to use his ovens once the baking is done for the day. Scrooge can see the desperate looks on the faces in the streets, and those who have any food to eat guard it carefully, scanning the crowd for anyone who may try to take it from them. When two dinner-carriers inadvertently bump into each other, a shouting match begins.

"Oy, watch where yer goin'!"

"Step off! You walked inter me path!"

Scrooge flinches as the argument escalates—he has seen this happen on the street before, and it often comes to blows.

But before the two can growl out another angry word, the giant reaches out and sprinkles what looks like water on their heads. Scrooge expects them to look up to try to find the source of the sprinkle, but the two simply blink and seem to see the other with new eyes. One holds out a hand, and they shake hands in friendship before walking together to the bakery, singing a rather off-key rendition of "Deck the Halls."

Ever since sin entered the world in the Garden of Eden, the earth has not been a peaceful place. From wars between countries to arguments between friends and family, peace is something that we all long for, but it often feels just beyond our grasp.

Generations before Jesus was born in Bethlehem, the prophet Isaiah foretold of His birth and described some of His characteristics. We read in Isaiah 9:

> *For a child is born to us, a son is given to us. The government will rest on his shoulders. And he will be called: Wonderful Counselor, Mighty God, Everlasting Father, Prince of Peace. (verse 6 NLT)*

Jesus, even before He was born, was proclaimed to bring peace to earth. And then in the first conversation about His birth—between angels and shepherds—we are told again of the peace He brings:

Suddenly a great company of the heavenly host appeared with the angel, praising God and saying, "Glory to God in the highest heaven, and on earth peace to those on whom his favor rests." (Luke 2:13–14 NIV)

This Christmas Jesus asks us to be an instrument of His peace. The holidays are a time of high stress and anxiety for some people, and when we see conflict rear its ugly head, we need to promote goodwill. Being a peacemaker may mean that you have to step out of your comfort zone. When Uncle Bob brings up a political topic at the dinner table that lights everybody up, be the person who steers the conversation to a more helpful and uplifting topic. When children are hopped up on sugar cookies and bouncing off the walls and you can't hear yourself think, instead of yelling, guide them to the playroom or the backyard to blow off some steam.

Peace can be found—at Christmas and every day of the year—if we let Christ's peace rule our hearts. Ask God in prayer for an extra dose of it this Christmas so that you have plenty to share with others.

"Peace I leave with you. My peace I give to you. I do not give peace to you as the world gives. Do not let your hearts be troubled or afraid."
JOHN 14:27 NLV

THE PROBLEM OF HYPOCRISY

"Is there a peculiar flavor in what you sprinkle from your torch?" asked Scrooge.

"There is. My own."

"Would it apply to any kind of dinner on this day?" asked Scrooge.

"To any kindly given. To a poor one most."

"Why to a poor one most?" asked Scrooge.

"Because it needs it most."

"Spirit," said Scrooge, after a moment's thought, "I wonder you, of all the beings in the many worlds about us, should desire to cramp these people's opportunities of innocent enjoyment."

"I!" cried the Spirit.

"You would deprive them of their means of dining every seventh day, often the only day on which they can be said to dine at all," said Scrooge, "wouldn't you?"

"I!" cried the Spirit.

"You seek to close these places on the Seventh Day," said Scrooge. "And it comes to the same thing."

"I seek!" exclaimed the Spirit.

"Forgive me if I am wrong. It has been done in your name, or at least in that of your family," said Scrooge.

"There are some upon this earth of yours," returned the Spirit, "who claim to know us, and who do their deeds of passion, pride, ill will, hatred, envy, bigotry, and selfishness in our name who are as strange to us, and all our kith and kin, as if they had never lived. Remember that, and charge their doings on themselves, not us."

Scrooge tries to make sense of what he sees the Ghost do as he continues to sprinkle something from his torch onto the poor and their meals. Maybe it is a special Christmas seasoning, Scrooge thinks. No, it is not a flavor enhancer, the Ghost says, but it is something that anyone can share—and it is especially meaningful to those in need.

Scrooge scratches his chin, still trying to understand fully. If it is Christian charity that the Ghost is spreading, then Ebenezer finds the Ghost's actions all the more confusing.

"It seems, Spirit, that you're just teasing these poor people with extra kindness on one day of the year. Isn't that rather cruel?" Scrooge muses, sure that he has caught the Ghost in a web of hypocrisy. "The rest of the year, you demand that the bakers close shop on Sundays to keep the Sabbath day holy. Once a week these people do not have cooked meals to satisfy your holiness."

"Do not confuse legalism with living out a real faith, Ebenezer," the Ghost says. "I am here to show your fellow men kindness on this day that is founded on love."

All throughout the Gospels, we see Jesus pressing back against highly educated religious sticklers—experts in Old Testament law—known as Pharisees. These men knew the ins and outs of God's commands and could quote, chapter and verse, every detail of the rules the Hebrew people had to follow to hope to be good enough to get into heaven. Jesus came to earth to bring a new way to live in faith, and the two most important laws are to (1) love God and (2) love others (Mark 12:30–31). Luke 13 tells a time when Jesus chose love over law:

One Sabbath day as Jesus was teaching in a synagogue, he saw a woman who had been crippled by an evil spirit. She had been bent double for eighteen years and was unable to stand up straight. When Jesus saw her, he called her over and said, "Dear woman, you are healed of your sickness!" Then he touched her, and instantly she could stand straight. How she praised God!

But the leader in charge of the synagogue was indignant that Jesus had healed her on the Sabbath day. "There are six days of the week for working," he said to the crowd. "Come on those days to be healed, not on the Sabbath."

But the Lord replied, "You hypocrites! Each of you works on the Sabbath day! Don't you untie your ox or your donkey from its stall on the Sabbath and lead it out for water? This dear woman, a daughter of Abraham, has been held in bondage by Satan for eighteen years. Isn't it right that she be released, even on the Sabbath?"

This shamed his enemies, but all the people rejoiced at the wonderful things he did. (verses 10–17 NLT)

When it comes down to it, people are more important to Jesus than anything else—and we should follow His example. This Christmas open your eyes to needs around you and fill those needs the way Jesus would, by seeing others for who they truly are: beloved individuals created in the image of God.

"A new command I give you: Love one another.
As I have loved you, so you must love one another.
By this everyone will know that you are my disciples,
if you love one another."
JOHN 13:34–35 NIV

SPRINKLE YOUR TORCH

And perhaps it was the pleasure the good Spirit had in showing off this power of his, or else it was his own kind, generous, hearty nature, and his sympathy with all poor men, that led him straight to Scrooge's clerk's; for there he went, and took Scrooge with him, holding to his robe and on the threshold of the door the Spirit smiled, and stopped to bless Bob Cratchit's dwelling with the sprinklings of his torch. Think of that! Bob had but fifteen "bob" a week himself; he pocketed on Saturdays but fifteen copies of his Christian name, and yet the Ghost of Christmas Present blessed his four-roomed house!

The Ghost of Christmas Present leads Ebenezer to a dodgy part of London, where the soot residue seems grimier and the dilapidated houses seem even more forlorn. Scrooge takes extra care not to touch or lean up against anything as he sees two rats scurry across an alleyway. The old man doesn't know it yet, but the Ghost has brought him to the home of Bob Cratchit. Scrooge furrows his brow as he takes in the house in front of him, wondering why anyone would choose such a hovel to live in. The tiny, dingy, drafty four-room structure houses Bob as well as his wife and large brood of children. To Ebenezer Scrooge, his clerk exists only at the firm of Scrooge & Marley, and although the old man knows, intellectually, that Bob has a life outside of work, he has never given a single thought to Bob Cratchit's circumstances.

The Spirit smiles as he sprinkles his torch on the entryway to the Cratchit home, an extra shake or two for good measure. It's such a meager setting for a celebration, but the feeling of unbridled Christmas hope invades every inch of the home and even spills out into the street—and the party hasn't even begun!

Christmas, more than any other time of the year, is when we spend time in other people's homes for dinners, parties, games, Christmas movies, and gift exchanges. If you have ever hosted such an event, you know the amount of time and effort that goes into a get-together. From shopping, baking, and cooking to decorating, cleaning, and preparing, a party to-do list can be long and time-consuming.

If you have been invited to the home of friends or family this year, you have the opportunity to be a blessing to them just as the Ghost blessed the Cratchits. You may not have a magical torch or a wand to wave to make a workload lighter, but there are simple things you can do to help. First, offer to—and if necessary, insist on—bringing something to the party. Maybe it will be an appetizer or a plate of cookies or a beverage or a pack of paper plates or some folding chairs or a special game to share. If there are small children in the home you will be visiting, offer to babysit prior to the event so the adults can focus on party preparation. In the days leading up to the party, pray for the host and hostess, asking a special blessing on them. And at the end of the festivities, help clean up the inevitable mess that results from a houseful of celebration.

Sprinkling your torch doesn't mean spending a lot of money. It doesn't mean doing something for someone else so that others will see how nice a person you are. Sprinkling your torch really means doing kind things for others that can be a blessing to them. Here is what the Bible has to say:

Remember to do good and help each other. Gifts like this please God. (Hebrews 13:16 NLV)

Dear children, let's not merely say that we love each other; let us show the truth by our actions. (1 John 3:17–18 NLT)

Giving that comes from a pure heart full of love for others is the very best Christmas present we can give—one that can bind friends and family together at Christmas and throughout the year.

"In everything I did, I showed you that by this kind of hard work we must help the weak, remembering the words the Lord Jesus himself said: 'It is more blessed to give than to receive.' "
ACTS 20:35 NIV

MAKING THE MOST OF WHAT WE HAVE

Then up rose Mrs. Cratchit, Cratchit's wife, dressed out but poorly in a twice-turned gown, but brave in ribbons, which are cheap and make a goodly show for sixpence; and she laid the cloth, assisted by Belinda Cratchit, second of her daughters, also brave in ribbons; while Master Peter Cratchit plunged a fork into the saucepan of potatoes, and getting the corners of his monstrous shirt collar (Bob's private property, conferred upon his son and heir in honor of the day) into his mouth, rejoiced to find himself so gallantly attired and yearned to show his linen in the fashionable Parks. And now two smaller Cratchits, boy and girl, came tearing in, screaming that outside the baker's they had smelled the goose, and known it for their own and, basking in luxurious thoughts of sage and onion, these young Cratchits danced about the table and exalted Master Peter Cratchit to the skies, while he (not proud, although his collars nearly choked him) blew the fire, until the slow potatoes, bubbling up, knocked loudly at the saucepan lid to be let out and peeled.

If there is one thing Mrs. Cratchit knows, it's how to stretch a penny. With seven mouths to feed, the grocer's bill is by far the family's biggest expense. But no one goes hungry, and in the very rare occurrence when the soup doesn't stretch as far as she thought it would, Mrs. Cratchit always makes sure everyone else has a full helping before she takes the smallest portion. She isn't very hungry, anyway.

Mrs. Cratchit's mother didn't leave her many worldly goods or riches, but she did leave her daughter with sewing skills that have added to her ability to clothe her husband and children. Every Cratchit dresses in hand-me-downs, but it's a secret that only the family knows for sure because Mother's magic with a needle and thread transforms old to new. The dress she wears this Christmas Day has been turned inside out twice now; each turning just required a little of her needle magic to make it look completely different. With the added touch of some festive ribbons (a rare treat), both Mrs. Cratchit and her daughter Belinda wear the spirit of the day happily. Even the oldest Cratchit son, Peter, wears a special shirt, a hand-me-down from his father. Mother tailored the sleeves and tail to fit the young man, but she couldn't do much with the starched collar, and it remains too large, making Peter's head look abnormally small. Still, in such finery, Peter takes care to keep his Christmas shirt clean as he checks the pot of boiled potatoes.

Have you experienced a Christmas when funds were tighter than normal? Financial setbacks come in many forms—job loss, economic downturn, medical expenses, natural disasters, unexpected home or car repairs. . .or even a combination of little things that add up to a big burden. Christmas comes with its own set of expenses, and even though it comes only once a year, when there are fewer dollars in the bank, you may find it hard to make ends meet.

If you are tempted to borrow money or use credit cards to pay for Christmas, remember that God's Word warns that a "borrower is slave to the lender" (Proverbs 22:7 NIV). Although going into debt is not a sin, it is a slippery slope that can chain you to financial problems longer than you plan.

John 6 records the story of Jesus feeding more than five thousand people with just five loaves of bread and two fish. Even Mrs. Cratchit would be impressed with those thrifty skills! Though Jesus could have simply thrown away the leftovers and done another miracle the next time the people were hungry, He shows us an example of frugality that we can follow in verse 12 (NLT):

> *After everyone was full, Jesus told his disciples, "Now gather the leftovers, so that nothing is wasted."*

This Christmas consider ways that you can save rather than spend. Like the Cratchits, make the most of what you have already, and rely on God's promise that He will take care of your needs (Philippians 4:19). Maybe a new Christmas outfit isn't in the budget, but the festive sweater from last year is still basically new. Get creative with gifts— make something with your own hands that you know the recipient will use. If you are living a Cratchit holiday this year, take heart—lean Christmases can result in some of the best memories, and you will have peace knowing that you are glorifying God with your financial choices.

> *At the moment I have all I need—and more! . . .*
> *And this same God who takes care of me will supply*
> *all your needs from his glorious riches, which have*
> *been given to us in Christ Jesus. Now all glory to*
> *God our Father forever and ever! Amen.*
> PHILIPPIANS 4:18–20 NLT

HOME FOR CHRISTMAS

"Here's Martha, mother!" cried the two young Cratchits. "Hurrah! There's such a goose, Martha!"

"Why, bless your heart alive, my dear, how late you are!" said Mrs. Cratchit, kissing her a dozen times and taking off her shawl and bonnet for her with officious zeal.

"We'd a deal of work to finish up last night," replied the girl, "and had to clear away this morning, Mother!"

"Well! Never mind so long as you are come," said Mrs. Cratchit. "Sit ye down before the fire, my dear, and have a warm, Lord bless ye!"

"No, no! There's Father coming," cried the two young Cratchits, who were everywhere at once. "Hide, Martha, hide!"

So Martha hid herself, and in came little Bob, the father, with at least three feet of comforter, exclusive of the fringe, hanging down before him, and his threadbare clothes darned up and brushed, to look seasonable, and Tiny Tim upon his shoulder. Alas for Tiny Tim, he bore a little crutch and had his limbs supported by an iron frame!

"Why, where's our Martha?" cried Bob Cratchit, looking round.

"Not coming," said Mrs. Cratchit.

"Not coming!" said Bob, with a sudden declension in his high spirits for he had been Tim's blood-horse all the way from church and had come home rampant. "Not coming upon Christmas Day!"

Martha didn't like to see him disappointed, if it were only a joke so she came out prematurely from behind the closet door and ran into his arms.

Martha, the eldest of the Cratchit children, was the first to fly the Cratchit nest just a few months ago when she secured a job as a milliner's apprentice in a fashionable part of London. Although she is paid only in room and board, it is a wonderful opportunity for Martha, and Mrs. Cratchit saves her darning money—just a few pennies she charges for any small seamstress work—to give to Martha for a treat now and then.

How Martha misses that tiny house and the shining faces in it! She doesn't get home as often as she would like, but London is a big city and transportation is not cheap. This morning she had hurried to finish nearly a whole day's work in order to arrive before the ceremonial goose carving.

Martha bursts in the door just as Mother gives up hope that her daughter will be joining them this holiday. The house erupts in excitement as the family is one more person closer to the celebration. Only missing yet are Father and Tiny Tim.

A jubilant shout from the young ones—Father is coming! The Cratchits, always game for a good-natured practical joke, convince Martha to hide so they can convince Father that Martha, sadly, won't be joining them. But Mother can barely get the words out when Martha sees the extreme disappointment on her father's face, and daughter immediately runs into Father's arms for a joyful Christmas reunion.

Christmas is a time for families to get together. You may spend more time with yours during the holidays than you do the rest of the year. That time is precious, but it may show some of the imperfections in your family as well. After all, families are made up of imperfect people.

Our heavenly Father knows that some of the very same people we love the most can sometimes drive us up the wall. They know which buttons to push, and they know the very best and the very worst about us. But if you're blessed to have a family that shares a similar faith, your family can be rooted in God's everlasting love:

> *"And you must love the LORD your God with all your heart, all your soul, and all your strength. And you must commit yourselves wholeheartedly to these commands that I am giving you today. Repeat them again and again to your children. Talk about them when you are at home and when you are on the road, when you are going to bed and when you are getting up. Tie them to your hands and wear them on your forehead as reminders. Write them on the doorposts of your house and on your gates." (Deuteronomy 6:5–9 NLT)*

This Christmas live out your faith with your family both in actions and in words. Talk about the things God has done for your family over the past year and pray together for the year to come. Love each other so that love can spill past the door of your home into the lives of others.

> *Above all, love each other deeply,*
> *because love covers over a multitude of sins.*
> 1 PETER 4:8 NIV

THE TINIEST OF TIMS

"And how did little Tim behave?" asked Mrs. Cratchit, when she had rallied Bob on his credulity, and Bob had hugged his daughter to his heart's content.

"As good as gold," said Bob, "and better. Somehow he gets thoughtful, sitting by himself so much, and thinks the strangest things you ever heard. He told me, coming home, that he hoped the people saw him in the church, because he was a cripple, and it might be pleasant to them to remember, upon Christmas Day, who made lame beggars walk and blind men see."

Bob's voice was tremulous when he told them this, and trembled more when he said that Tiny Tim was growing strong and hearty.

His active little crutch was heard upon the floor, and back came Tiny Tim before another word was spoken, escorted by his brother and sister to his stool beside the fire.

Mrs. Cratchit knew her pregnancy was ending too soon, but there was nothing she could do to stop the labor pains, so her youngest child came into the world with a ready-made nickname—Tiny Tim. Life was a challenge for Timothy Cratchit from the moment he drew his first labored breath. But the Cratchits rejoiced over the blessing of a new little soul to love, and Bob fairly jigged through the streets on his way to the Scrooge & Marley office the morning after Tim's birth.

The stretch of colic that plagued Tiny Tim seemed like it may never end—mother and father taking turns rocking the infant and humming soothing tunes into the wee morning hours. In the peaceful cooing moments, Tim's generosity with smiles more than made up for the sleepless nights.

Tim grew, as infants do, but he continued to develop more slowly than the other babes in the neighborhood. While other tykes soon were daring to pull themselves to their feet and dash off in a toddle-run, Tiny Tim seemed content to sit on the kitchen floor and bang a wooden spoon on the rough planks to his own syncopated rhythm as Mother did the baking. She tried not to worry, instead thanking God for the bright eyes and sweet countenance of her youngest child.

As Tim approached his third birthday, his small frame seemed to become more bent and strange. Through sheer force of will, he learned to walk short distances by dragging the more pitifully bent leg behind the other. He spent most of his time perched on his favorite stool, helping Mother prepare a meal in his own childlike way or watching his siblings in active play.

Just before Tiny Tim's fourth birthday, the family finally scraped together enough money for a single visit from the doctor, who fitted him for a leg brace and crutch. The doctor put on a brave face for the boy, but in hushed tones with Tim's parents, he shared the reality: Tim would eventually weaken as his bones deteriorated and would finally succumb to a childhood death.

Nearly a year has passed since Tim's diagnosis, and Tim's ability with the brace and crutch is unmatched in all of London. Still, he tires easily and the rattle in his chest flares up whenever he walks too far or gets too excited, so Bob carries his small son perched high on his shoulder whenever the lad will let him, hailing him as the king of England himself. Mother and Father marvel at the wisdom that comes from the lips of one so young. If God intended Tiny Tim to be a blessing to the Cratchit family, he has been—a hundred times over.

Other than Scrooge himself, Tiny Tim might be the most memorable character in Dickens's story. Although he appears in only one scene, his story is so compelling, so heart-wrenching, that we can't help but feel for the boy and his family. And his illness and physical struggles make Tim's joyful attitude all the more amazing!

When we or someone we love suffers physical pain or illness, often the last emotion we feel is joy. Fear, stress, doubt, loneliness, medical expenses, and daily struggles all add up to a burden that can feel impossible to carry. And if the issue is chronic or terminal, hope seems useless, so why bother?

The truth is, God will provide joy, hope, peace, and even contentment in any situation if we allow Him—even one as dire as Tiny Tim's. The apostle Paul wrote of his own physical problem in 2 Corinthians 12. He asked God to heal him three times, and God answered him:

> *"I am all you need. I give you My loving-favor. My power works best in weak people." I am happy to be weak and have troubles so I can have Christ's power in me. (verse 9 NLV)*

When we live our daily lives acknowledging our weakness and need of God's love and power, He is faithful to work mightily. That may mean healing one day, but it also may mean that He will show us a different outcome—one that demonstrates His all-encompassing love through our story. Tiny Tim understood that idea when he told Bob he hoped the people at church would be reminded of Jesus' miracles when they saw him at Christmas services.

Can your struggles be a testimony to the power of God? If you are going through a tough time now, ask God for a new understanding of His work in you and your family. He hears your prayers!

We can rejoice, too, when we run into problems and trials, for we know that they help us develop endurance. And endurance develops strength of character, and character strengthens our confident hope of salvation. And this hope will not lead to disappointment. For we know how dearly God loves us, because he has given us the Holy Spirit to fill our hearts with his love.
ROMANS 5:3–5 NLT

SIMPLE JOYS

At last the dishes were set on, and grace was said. It was succeeded by a breathless pause, as Mrs. Cratchit, looking slowly all along the carving knife, prepared to plunge it in the breast, but when she did, and when the long-expected gush of stuffing issued forth, one murmur of delight arose all round the board, and even Tiny Tim, excited by the two young Cratchits, beat on the table with the handle of his knife, and feebly cried "Hurrah!"

There never was such a goose. Bob said he didn't believe there ever was such a goose cooked. Its tenderness and flavor, size and cheapness, were the themes of universal admiration. Eked out by applesauce and mashed potatoes, it was a sufficient dinner for the whole family; indeed, as Mrs. Cratchit said with great delight (surveying one small atom of a bone upon the dish), they hadn't ate it all at last! Yet every one had enough, and the youngest Cratchits in particular were steeped in sage and onion to the eyebrows! . . .

Oh, a wonderful pudding! Bob Cratchit said—and calmly, too—that he regarded it as the greatest success achieved by Mrs. Cratchit since their marriage. Mrs. Cratchit said that, now the weight was off her mind, she would confess she had her doubts about the quantity of flour. Everybody had something to say about it, but nobody said or thought it was at all a small pudding for a large family. It would have been flat heresy to do so. Any Cratchit would have blushed to hint at such a thing. . . .

There was nothing of high mark in this. They were not a handsome family, they were not well dressed, their

shoes were far from being waterproof, their clothes were
scanty, and Peter might have known, and very likely
did, the inside of a pawnbroker's. But they were happy,
grateful, pleased with one another, and contented with
the time.

Every year in the weeks leading up to Christmas, each member of the Cratchit family looked forward to the coming Christmas feast. Yes, they thought about it and even daydreamed about it, but they also literally dreamed of it while they slumbered.

Bob dreamed of the Christmas punch and what he might do this year to improve upon last year's batch. Mrs. Cratchit's dream of the Christmas pudding may be better described as a nightmare as the dessert in her slumber always seemed to deflate as soon as it was removed from the copper. Still, her dream husband and children always hailed it as a culinary masterpiece and seemed to enjoy it all the same, making her heart happy. Martha dreamed of her very own plate piled high with only mashed potatoes and gravy, and Peter once dreamed of a washtub filled with applesauce for bathing in. Belinda once dreamed of a tree—miraculously filled with *roasted* chestnuts on Christmas morning. And the two younger Cratchits each dreamed of eating so much sage and onion stuffing that they got sick. And Tim—dreamtime Tim only had eyes for the goose. That wonderful bird of white meat and dark, and the best part that the family gladly saved for their youngest—the giblets.

No Cratchit leaves the Christmas feast table disappointed,

and all agree that this year's topped all previous holiday dinners. Tim wonders aloud if they could ever hope to match it again. As the family gathers around the hearth to sing carols and play a few games, the glow of Christmas envelops their hearts and shines on their faces.

The picture Dickens paints here of the Cratchit family Christmas is one of contentment. With little money for daily extravagances, Bob and family look forward to Christmas with such anticipation and excitement that the joy they feel with spending time together, eating special food, and breaking their normal routine of work, is nothing short of a short vacation from reality. And each person seems to cherish every moment of it.

Christmas is a time of high excitement, complete with surprise gifts, dazzling decorations, out-of-town guests, special events, and truly delicious food. All of these things are great, but if we're not careful, our celebrations can get out of control as we try to make each year bigger and brighter and more impressive (and expensive). When we are in a constant cycle of upping the stakes, we may find that we are never able to find contentment in the holiday—leaving us disappointed.

Whether you have all the money in the world to spend on Christmas or your Christmas is looking a bit lean, you can choose contentment just as the apostle Paul did when he wrote to the Philippian church, encouraging them to do the same:

I have learned how to be content with whatever I have. I know how to live on almost nothing or with everything. I have learned the secret of living in every situation, whether it is with a full stomach or empty, with plenty or little. For I can do everything through Christ, who gives me strength. (Philippians 4:11–13 NLT)

There's a reason why Christmas is the most wonderful time of the year. The birth of the baby who would make the way for us to live eternally with God is the best reason to celebrate! This season shift your focus from the temporary trappings of the holiday and find new contentment in the everlasting hope of Christ. You will find your celebration will be all the merrier!

"Don't store up treasures here on earth, where moths eat them and rust destroys them, and where thieves break in and steal. Store your treasures in heaven, where moths and rust cannot destroy, and thieves do not break in and steal. Wherever your treasure is, there the desires of your heart will also be."
MATTHEW 6:19–21 NLT

"GOD BLESS US, EVERY ONE!"

At last the dinner was all done, the cloth was cleared, the hearth swept, and the fire made up. The compound in the jug being tasted and considered perfect, apples and oranges were put upon the table, and a shovelful of chestnuts on the fire. Then all the Cratchit family drew round the hearth in what Bob Cratchit called a circle, meaning half a one, and at Bob Cratchit's elbow stood the family display of glass—two tumblers and a custard cup without a handle.

These held the hot stuff from the jug, however, as well as golden goblets would have done; and Bob served it out with beaming looks, while the chestnuts on the fire sputtered and crackled noisily. Then Bob proposed:

"A merry Christmas to all, my dears. God bless us!"

Which all the family reechoed.

"God bless us, every one!" said Tiny Tim, the last of all.

Tiny Tim sits on his stool, tasked by Bob to guard a paper bag filled with chestnuts, as the Cratchit women clear away the dinner dishes and the Cratchit men make quick work of rebuilding and stoking the fire.

As the family of eight settles in for a cozy afternoon, Tim relinquishes the chestnuts to Father, who expertly places them in the coal shovel to roast over the hottest part of the fire. Mother retrieves a current project from her sewing basket—adding a new ruffle to one of Martha's hand-me-down pinafores for Belinda. Peter helps the younger ones peel their oranges, and a lovely scent of citrus fills the room, mingling with the lemon in Bob's Christmas punch, kept warm near the fire. Martha and Belinda make quick work of putting away dishes and removing their aprons before sitting, each grinning at the other about what's coming next.

With such pomp and ceremony as fit for a king's coronation, Bob Cratchit lines the mantel with the family's finest china—two glass tumblers and a handleless custard cup—before uncorking the jug and testing the Christmas punch. He proclaims the punch to be fit for consumption. Tipping the jug carefully so as not to spill a drop, Bob distributes the first portions equally among the containers. With only three cups, the first sips rotate among the family from year to year, and this year the honor goes to the three youngest Cratchits. But first the traditional toast from the head of the house, kind and caring father, husband, provider, and friend lifts the pitiful custard cup as if it were the finest chalice in King Arthur's royal treasury. His heartfelt Christmas blessing fills the hearts of each person in the room—six voices returning the toast heartily.

Bob hands the custard cup to Tiny Tim for the first drink, squeezing his tiny hand gently around the cup to make sure his son has a firm grip. Tim smiles warmly as he looks into the kind eyes of his beloved father and echoes back in a clear, strong voice with no hint of the rattle in his chest, "God bless us, every one!"

Even with the joy of Christmas Day, the reality of Tiny Tim's illness is never far from the minds of the Cratchit family. It would be easy for them to dwell on Tim's suffering and make everything about how sad the whole situation is, but Tim doesn't dwell on it, so why should the rest of the family?

Tim Cratchit has so much to teach us. For a sickly boy who is undoubtedly stared at, pitied, and likely mocked by others, Tiny Tim has a heart only for others. We see this in his thoughts and actions, and when Bob uttered a loving Christmas blessing for his family, Tiny Tim repeated the blessing but included the prayer even more broadly—asking God's blessing on "every one."

We all are guilty of being self-centered, especially when we're going through tough times. It's easy to fall into the trap of believing the world revolves around *me* and *my problems* and *how to make it better.* But the Bible tells us to focus on others rather than ourselves:

> *Don't just pretend to love others. Really love them.*
> *Hate what is wrong. Hold tightly to what is good. Love*
> *each other with genuine affection, and take delight in*
> *honoring each other.* (Romans 12:9–10 NLT)

Once again we see that living out a genuine faith in any circumstance comes down to loving others. First Timothy 2:1 urges us to pray for all people and ask God to help them and thank God for their role in our lives. Tiny Tim, wise beyond his years, understood this very thing. Follow his example and experience true selflessness that pleases our heavenly Father.

> *Love is patient and kind. Love is not jealous or boastful*
> *or proud or rude. It does not demand its own way. It is*
> *not irritable, and it keeps no record of being wronged.*
> *It does not rejoice about injustice but rejoices whenever*
> *the truth wins out. Love never gives up, never loses faith,*
> *is always hopeful, and endures through every circumstance.*
> 1 Corinthians 13:4–7 NLT

THE VACANT SEAT

[Tiny Tim] sat very close to his father's side, upon his little stool. Bob held his withered little hand in his, as if he loved the child and wished to keep him by his side, and dreaded that he might be taken from him.

"Spirit," said Scrooge, with an interest he had never felt before, "tell me if Tiny Tim will live."

"I see a vacant seat," replied the Ghost, "in the poor chimney corner, and a crutch without an owner, carefully preserved. If these shadows remain unaltered by the future, the child will die."

"No, no," said Scrooge. "Oh, no, kind Spirit! Say he will be spared."

"If these shadows remain unaltered by the future, none other of my race," returned the Ghost, "will find him here. What then? If he be like to die, he had better do it, and decrease the population."

Scrooge hung his head to hear his own words quoted by the Spirit and was overcome with penitence and grief.

As Bob Cratchit sits in his customary chair next to Tiny Tim, the boy struggles to scoot his small stool closer to his father. With a quick motion, Bob, although not a large man himself, easily moves lad and stool up against his own chair before wrapping an arm around his youngest son.

Belinda Cratchit, unarguably the best singer in the family, begins a sweet rendition of "Silent Night" in her alto voice, and the family joins. A cough catches in Tim's chest at the "Round yon virgin" bit, and he gasps for breath while trying to clear the rattle. Bob gently pats his back while continuing to sing, and Tim joins in again on "Sleep in heavenly peace," slipping his tiny, withered hand into his father's strong one as they start in on verse two.

Bob feels his voice begin to quake, just as the shepherds did in the presence of the angel, but despite the extreme sadness that grips his heart, he wills his voice to steady and hugs his small son closer to him, thanking heaven for the time they have been given together.

Something stirs inside Ebenezer Scrooge as he watches the scene before him—a sensation he has never felt before. Could it be concern about someone other than himself, or is it simply morbid curiosity? Either way, Scrooge asks the Ghost of Christmas Present about Tiny Tim's future.

The Ghost, although not much of a fortune-teller, can see the boy's future as plain as day. If nothing changes, Timothy Cratchit will die before next Christmas.

The Ghost's answer makes Scrooge realize he does, in fact, care about what happens to Tiny Tim, and the old man pleads with the Spirit to spare his young life. But that wish is not within the Spirit's power to grant. Instead, the Ghost repeats back to Scrooge his own coldhearted logic that if Tim is going to die, he had better do it so there is one less person making the world more crowded than it needs to be. The words pierce through Scrooge's head and heart, and he has never felt so sorry in his life.

Have you ever considered that helping someone else is more than just a nice thing to do that makes us feel good? Jesus tells us in Luke 6:31 to treat others the way we want to be treated. Kind things we do to others may show immediate results, but they may also set off a chain reaction of God's work that we may never see. Imagine it: even the smallest blessing or kindness we show someone in need may alter that person's future in a way that actually saves his or her physical or spiritual life.

The apostle Paul in Philippians 2 explains how our sacrifices for others, in a small way, reflect the sacrifice Jesus made for us:

> *Don't look out only for your own interests, but take an interest in others, too.*
> *You must have the same attitude that Christ Jesus had. Though he was God, he did not think of equality with God as something to cling to. Instead, he gave up his divine privileges; he took the humble position of a slave and was born as a human being. When he appeared in human form, he humbled himself in obedience to God and died a criminal's death on a cross. (verses 4–8 NLT)*

Only God knows what will happen when we make the decision to help someone, but He can show us what He wants us to do through His Holy Spirit who lives in our hearts. Don't ignore the prodding of the Spirit, especially at Christmas. Do the kindness for someone else that can change the course of that person's future for good.

> *Finally, all of you should be of one mind. Sympathize with each other. Love each other as brothers and sisters. Be tenderhearted, and keep a humble attitude.*
> 1 PETER 3:8 NLT

"THE FOUNDER OF THE FEAST, INDEED!"

"Mr. Scrooge!" said Bob; "I'll give you Mr. Scrooge, the founder of the feast!"

"The founder of the feast, indeed!" cried Mrs. Cratchit, reddening. "I wish I had him here. I'd give him a piece of my mind to feast upon, and I hope he'd have a good appetite for it."

"My dear," said Bob, "the children! Christmas Day."

"It should be Christmas Day, I am sure," said she, "on which one drinks the health of such an odious, stingy, hard, unfeeling man as Mr. Scrooge. You know he is, Robert! Nobody knows it better than you do, poor fellow!"

"My dear," was Bob's mild answer, "Christmas Day."

"I'll drink his health for your sake, and the day's," said Mrs. Cratchit, "not for his. Long life to him! A merry Christmas and a happy New Year! He'll be very merry and very happy, I have no doubt!"

The children drank the toast after her. It was the first of their proceedings which had no heartiness in it. Tiny Tim drank it last of all, but he didn't care twopence for it. Scrooge was the ogre of the family. The mention of his name cast a dark shadow on the party, which was not dispelled for full five minutes.

A second round of Christmas punch means another toast, and Bob Cratchit stands and raises his glass (this time one of the tumblers) to recognize his employer, one Mr.

Ebenezer Scrooge, as the provider of their delicious meal.

Now Mrs. Cratchit is known among family and friends for her good, gentle nature—a mother to all who have need of one—who never has an unkind word for anyone. . .except for Mr. Scrooge. For too many years she has seen her poor husband overworked, ill-treated, and abused for a meager wage that barely keeps the family out of the workhouses. But Bob takes pride in his job and ability to provide for the family, so Mrs. Cratchit keeps her feelings to herself—as much as she can. Seeing her beloved husband raise a glass to the evil tyrant Scrooge lights a rage in her chest that she cannot extinguish before her true feelings erupt from her lips.

The looks of surprise on her children's faces immediately bring a blush to her cheeks. She is embarrassed at the outburst, but she is not sorry. It needed to be said. The children must understand how hard their father works for the roof over their heads, clothes on their backs, and food in their stomachs. A hot tear slips down her cheek and she catches it with a quick fingertip.

She hears a soft rebuke—a voice of reason pleading for charity on Christmas Day—from her beloved husband. She looks up into his loving eyes and accepts the glass from his outstretched hand and raises it before choosing her words carefully.

"We need Mr. Scrooge to remain healthy, so I will drink to his health. He has so much that he had better be happy and merry this Christmas." Her words are layered thick with sarcasm, but this is the closest thing she can mutter to a true toast before sipping a bit of punch. The children follow her lead, and although each one drinks to Mr. Scrooge in turn, none mean it in their heart of hearts.

It's hard to blame Mrs. Cratchit for her righteous indignation during Bob's toast to Mr. Scrooge. The truth is that Scrooge *has been* and *continues to be* terrible to her husband, and it is often more difficult to deal with someone bullying those we love than it is to deal with being bullied ourselves.

Mrs. Cratchit has been holding a grudge against Ebenezer Scrooge for years, and it has slowly taken root in her heart. Someone once said that holding a grudge is like drinking poison and hoping the other person will die. It's true that any ill feelings Mrs. Cratchit holds against her husband's boss are doing nothing to hurt Scrooge. Instead, her attitude casts a shadow on her own family's Christmas celebration.

Bob, on the other hand, knows exactly how mistreated he is by Mr. Scrooge, but he has somehow figured out a way to forgive him and look past the hardships he suffers at the hand of his employer. Bob's conscious decision to continue to be good to Ebenezer Scrooge mirrors what Jesus tells us to do in Matthew 5:

> *"You have heard the law that says, 'Love your neighbor' and hate your enemy. But I say, love your enemies! Pray for those who persecute you! In that way, you will be acting as true children of your Father in heaven. For he gives his sunlight to both the evil and the good, and he sends rain on the just and the unjust alike." (verses 43–45 NLT)*

Who is the Scrooge in your life? Who could you never raise a glass to and toast with Christmas punch? God invites that person to be His child just as you are His child. Pray and ask God to open your heart to your Scrooge. Pray blessings for that person's health, family, and spiritual life. Then you will be acting with a pure heart that God desires from all his children.

Do not be overcome by evil,
but overcome evil with good.
ROMANS 12:21 NIV

"I AM SORRY FOR HIM"

"He's a comical old fellow," said Scrooge's nephew, "that's the truth; and not so pleasant as he might be. However, his offenses carry their own punishment, and I have nothing to say against him."

"I'm sure he is very rich, Fred," hinted Scrooge's niece. "At least you always tell me so."

"What of that, my dear?" said Scrooge's nephew. "His wealth is of no use to him. He doesn't do any good with it. He doesn't make himself comfortable with it. He hasn't the satisfaction of thinking—ha, ha, ha!—that he is ever going to benefit us with it."

"I have no patience with him," observed Scrooge's niece. Scrooge's nieces' sisters, and all the other ladies, expressed the same opinion.

"Oh, I have!" said Scrooge's nephew. "I am sorry for him: I couldn't be angry with him if I tried. Who suffers by his ill whims? Himself, always. Here, he takes it into his head to dislike us, and he won't come and dine with us. What's the consequence? He doesn't lose much of a dinner."...

"I was only going to say," said Scrooge's nephew, "that the consequence of his taking a dislike to us and not making merry with us, is, as I think, that he loses some pleasant moments, which could do him no harm. I am sure he loses pleasanter companions than he can find in his own thoughts, either in his moldy old office or his dusty chambers. I mean to give him the same chance every year, whether he likes it or not, for I pity him. He may rail at Christmas till he dies, but he can't help

thinking better of it—I defy him—if he finds me going there, in good temper, year after year, and saying, 'Uncle Scrooge, how are you?' If it only puts him in the vein to leave his poor clerk fifty pounds, that's something, and I think I shook him, yesterday."

Fred and his wife host a wonderful holiday party every year, there's no question about that. Family and friends eagerly await the invitation to their house for Christmas Day celebrations. The only damper on the whole event is that the name Ebenezer Scrooge is bound to come up in conversation at some point. What is Fred's fascination with the old skinflint anyway?

As a tray of cookies and fudge is passed around the room, Fred recounts his Christmas Eve visit to Scrooge & Marley, and even though it seems ol' Ebenezer's heart is just as cold and dormant as it ever was, Fred still hopes that every year, with every interaction he has with his uncle, he might see a sign of a spring thaw.

But still, as Fred's guests roll their eyes at and click their tongues in pity for the old codger, Fred can't help but love his mother's brother and want the best for him. Truthfully, his heart aches for his uncle Ebenezer. The old man doesn't even realize how miserable he is. If only he would open up his heart to the opportunities to show a bit of kindness and accept a bit of love.

There are times in all our lives when we need to make a change. And sometimes we are guilty of being so self-centered that we can't see the problems that are obvious to the people around us who love us. Fred, wise beyond his years, sees great potential in his uncle's life—the potential to do good with his finances, the potential to form strong relationships with friends and family—and Fred continues to try to knock down the wall that Scrooge has built. We don't know for sure, but Fred likely reaches out to his uncle more than just once a year at Christmas. He may find excuses to pop in to the Scrooge & Marley countinghouse on a regular basis to invite Scrooge to a Sunday dinner or a birthday celebration. Every invitation (so far) has been met with a no, but Fred won't give up on his uncle.

Maybe you have a lost cause in your life this Christmas. These are the people you have reached out to over and over again with God's love, but they are not interested and may even be hostile toward hearing about it. But even if you have come to a point where you think your lost cause may be truly lost, God can soften the hearts of even those farthest away.

Our all-powerful Father God can and does work behind the scenes in ways that we don't see when it comes to reaching lost people. And sometimes it takes years for us to see those results. God's timing is a mystery to us, but the Bible assures us that He is working in the lives of lost causes:

The Lord isn't really being slow about his promise, as some people think. No, he is being patient for your sake. He does not want anyone to be destroyed, but wants everyone to repent. (2 Peter 3:9 NLT)

Jesus tells a story in Luke 15 about a man who has a hundred sheep and loses one, and the man leaves the remaining ninety-nine to search for the lost one until he finds it. A huge celebration ensues once that single sheep is found. Jesus goes on to say, "There is more joy in heaven over one lost sinner who repents and returns to God than over ninety-nine others who are righteous and haven't strayed away" (verse 7 NLT). Christ invites us to search for these lost sheep, these Scrooges, too. And the celebration that ensues in heaven and in our hearts will be even better than the Christmas party at Fred's house.

The faithful love of the LORD never ends!
His mercies never cease. Great is his faithfulness;
his mercies begin afresh each morning.
LAMENTATIONS 3:22–23 NLT

A FRIEND CAN BE A MIRROR

"Here is a new game," said Scrooge. *"One half-hour, Spirit, only one!"*

It was a game called Yes and No, where Scrooge's nephew had to think of something, and the rest must find out what, he only answering to their questions yes or no, as the case was. The brisk fire of questioning to which he was exposed elicited from him that he was thinking of an animal, a live animal, rather a disagreeable animal, a savage animal, an animal that growled and grunted sometimes, and talked sometimes, and lived in London, and walked about the streets, and wasn't made a show of, and wasn't led by anybody, and didn't live in a menagerie, and was never killed in a market, and was not a horse, or an ass, or a cow, or a bull, or a tiger, or a dog, or a pig, or a cat, or a bear. At every fresh question that was put to him, this nephew burst into a fresh roar of laughter and was so inexpressibly tickled that he was obliged to get up off the sofa and stamp. At last the plump sister, falling into a similar state, cried out:

"I have found it out! I know what it is, Fred! I know what it is!"

"What is it?" cried Fred.

"It's your uncle Scro-o-o-oge!"

Which it certainly was. Admiration was the universal sentiment, though some objected that the reply to "Is it a bear?" ought to have been "Yes," inasmuch as an answer in the negative was sufficient to have diverted their thoughts from Mr. Scrooge, supposing they had ever had any tendency that way.

"He has given us plenty of merriment, I am sure," said Fred, "and it would be ungrateful not to drink his health. Here is a glass of mulled wine ready to our hand at the moment and I say, 'Uncle Scrooge!' "

"Well! Uncle Scrooge!" they cried. "A merry Christmas and a happy New Year to the old man, whatever he is!" said Scrooge's nephew. "He wouldn't take it from me, but may he have it, nevertheless. Uncle Scrooge!"

At last Fred announces that it is time for games, and the partygoers enjoy rounds of forfeits and blindman's buff that nearly result in the destruction of an heirloom vase. Scrooge loses himself in the scene and nearly forgets that what he is seeing are merely shadows of events, laughing as heartily as the rest of the room at the merriment.

The Ghost points to the clock on the mantel, as Fred announces a new game called Yes or No. Scrooge pleads for just a half hour more, and the Ghost, weary with age, nods slightly before taking a seat for a snooze.

The questions come rapid-fire from the guests, and Fred answers them quickly. Whatever animal it is that he is thinking of quickly falls into the category of something very unpleasant—something no one wants. Scrooge's mind whirs. If it lives in and walks the streets of London, maybe it is a rat. Those pests were the scourge of the city these days and seemed to spread filth wherever they went.

An outburst from a guest brings Scrooge back to the scene. Why was she shrieking his own name? The other guests explode in laughter, and the light slowly dawns on Ebenezer. *He* is the answer to the riddle.

Scrooge's head falls and his shoulders slump at the realization. Is this really what his family thinks of him? And if this is what Fred—the one person who cares for Scrooge—believes, what must others think?

Have you ever had a friend tell you something about yourself that you didn't like to hear? Maybe that friend revealed something about your attitude or the words you use that made you stop and think. Proverbs tells us that friends can act as mirrors, even when it hurts to hear the hard truth:

An open rebuke is better than hidden love! Wounds from a sincere friend are better than many kisses from an enemy. (27:5–6 NLT)

As iron sharpens iron, so a friend sharpens a friend. (27:17 NLT)

Ebenezer Scrooge has spent the majority of his life closing himself off from others. Even as a child, he had a strained relationship with his father, and similar issues popped up later with his fiancée, Belle, so now he keeps all his relationships (if you can call them that) at arm's length. Do you have friends who can be your mirror? Friends who can tell you when you're doing something you shouldn't be doing or heading down a path that will lead to nothing good?

Pray and ask God to strengthen your relationships so that you can accept reflection and reflect back to others, always in love.

Instead, we will speak the truth in love, growing in every way more and more like Christ.
EPHESIANS 4:15 NLT

IGNORANCE AND WANT

From the foldings of his robe, [the Ghost] brought two children, wretched, abject, frightful, hideous, miserable. They knelt down at his feet, and clung upon the outside of his garment.

"O Man! look here! Look, look, down here!" exclaimed the Ghost.

They were a boy and girl. Yellow, meager, ragged, scowling, wolfish; but prostrate, too, in their humility. Where graceful youth should have filled their features out, and touched them with its freshest tints, a stale and shriveled hand, like that of age, had pinched and twisted them, and pulled them into shreds. Where angels might have sat enthroned, devils lurked, and glared out menacing. No change, no degradation, no perversion of humanity, in any grade, through all the mysteries of wonderful creation, has monsters half so horrible and dread.

Scrooge started back, appalled. Having them shown to him in this way, he tried to say they were fine children, but the words choked themselves, rather than be parties to a lie of such enormous magnitude.

"Spirit! Are they yours?" Scrooge could say no more.

"They are man's," said the Spirit, looking down upon them. "And they cling to me, appealing from their fathers. This boy is Ignorance. This girl is Want. Beware of them both, and all of their degree, but most of all beware this boy, for on his brow I see that written which is Doom, unless the writing be erased. Deny it!" cried the Spirit, stretching out its hand toward the city. "Slander those who tell it ye! Admit it for your factious purposes, and make it worse! And bide the end!"

"Have they no refuge or resource?" cried Scrooge.

"Are there no prisons?" said the Spirit, turning on him for the last time with his own words. "Are there no workhouses?"

The bell struck twelve.

The Ghost tells Scrooge that their time together is almost done. As the clock rings three-quarters past eleven, Ebenezer sees a strange movement under the Spirit's robe and asks what it is.

The Ghost pulls back the folds of his robe to reveal two desperate, frightful figures—a small boy and girl—more animal-like than childlike. They are dirty, disheveled, skeleton-thin, and wild-eyed, and Scrooge startles and jumps away from the children while pitying them terribly, and asks the Spirit who they are.

The boy, the Ghost says, is Ignorance. And the girl is Want. Both should be avoided, but Ignorance is much worse because he leads to a destructive end.

"But do they not have anyone to take care of them, poor children?" Scrooge wonders aloud, seeking the Spirit's eyes for some reassurance.

The Ghost's gaze pierces Scrooge as the miser hears a familiar rebuttal: "Are there no prisons? Are there no workhouses?" Scrooge's heart pounds in his ears as he hears the clock strike twelve and the Ghost and child creatures disappear into the mist.

Scrooge's time with the Ghosts of Christmas Past and Present brought Scrooge moments of both joy and sadness, but as their time came to an end, the Spirit wanted to make sure that he made his point perfectly clear to Ebenezer: *There are many needs in this world that you can do something about. The worst thing you can do is turn a blind eye to these needs.*

The same is true for us today. There are needs everywhere—from just across the street to all the way across the world. It's easy for us to become blind to others' needs when all of our needs (and many of our wants) are taken care of. We may fall into the trap of thinking that if we're okay, then the rest of the world is okay, too.

But there will always be needs and ways for each of us to help someone else. Throughout scripture God tells us that as people of faith, it is our responsibility to take care of those needs:

> *"Give generously to the poor, not grudgingly, for the LORD your God will bless you in everything you do. There will always be some in the land who are poor. That is why I am commanding you to share freely with the poor and with other Israelites in need." (Deuteronomy 15:10–11 NLT)*

> *"If you have two coats, give one to him who has none. If you have food, you must share some." (Luke 3:11 NLV)*

This Christmas ask God to open your eyes and your heart to needs around you. Ask God to remove all ignorance from your life and make you sensitive to ways you can fill a need—to spread His love to a world that is in desperate need of His love and grace.

> *If you help the poor, you are lending to the LORD—and he will repay you!*
> PROVERBS 19:17 NLT

Stave Four

LEARNING FROM OUR DIFFERENCES

*As the last stroke ceased to vibrate, [Scrooge]
remembered the prediction of old Jacob Marley, and,
lifting up his eyes, beheld a solemn Phantom, draped
and hooded, coming like a mist along the ground
toward him.*

*"Ghost of the Future!" he exclaimed, "I fear you
more than any specter I have seen. But as I know your
purpose is to do me good, and as I hope to live to be
another man from what I was, I am prepared to bear
you company, and do it with a thankful heart. Will you
not speak to me?"*

*It gave him no reply. The hand was pointed straight
before them.*

*"Lead on," said Scrooge. "Lead on! The night is
waning fast, and it is precious time to me, I know. Lead
on, Spirit!"*

As the bell tolls the last stroke of midnight, Ebenezer looks up to see a figure altogether frightening: a ghost wearing a dark, hooded cloak that reaches all the way to the ground. Squinting, Scrooge looks for any sign of life from beneath the cloak—a form of a body or eyes gazing from beneath the hood or a hint of steam from warm breath in the frigid night air—but he sees none coming from the Ghost.

Ebenezer clasps his shaking hands and clears his throat nervously as the Ghost moves toward him—seemingly floating along the surface of the earth, the ragged edges of the cloak's hem skimming the ground. He calls out to the Ghost and acknowledges his fear, but he is ready to learn whatever it is the Phantom has in store. The Spirit doesn't reply but raises an arm to point straight ahead with a ghoulishly skeletal finger.

"Lead on!" Ebenezer croaks out from a throat that's tight with fear. If the Ghost isn't going to talk, Scrooge will fill the awkward silence with even more awkward talk.

At this point in the story, Scrooge is somewhat of an expert at interacting with ghosts. He is no longer in denial about the reality of what is going on in front of him, and he has already realized that these ghosts that Jacob Marley promised have actually taught him a thing or two. As the jovial, kindhearted Ghost of Christmas Present leaves and ushers in this final Spirit—a sort of Grim Reaper twin— Scrooge is ready to follow wherever he may lead.

It's been a long time coming, but Scrooge has finally started to let go of the pride that kept him from fully learning the lessons from the earlier Ghosts. Dickens doesn't tell us whether it's from partial fear or actual full surrender that Scrooge willingly looks for and then follows the Ghost of Christmas Yet to Come, but either way, it's quite a change in attitude.

The fact that Scrooge isn't putting up a fight with this Ghost might be his first real display of wisdom in our story. He is ready to lay aside his wishes in order to learn what the Ghost has to teach him.

Here is what the book of Proverbs says about the relationship between wisdom and pride:

When pride comes, then comes shame, but wisdom is with those who have no pride. (11:2 NLV)

Are you ever guilty of thinking that you already know everything there is to know about a situation? Maybe it's a decision you need to make or a problem you need to work through. Whatever it is, you have it all under control and know exactly what you need to do. That's when pride sneaks in and pushes wisdom out.

God wants us to humble ourselves and acknowledge that we *don't* know everything. He will show us, through scripture and through counsel of godly friends and family, what He wants us to know—what is truly wise.

Are you willing to let go of your pride to let God's wisdom guide your life? Ebenezer Scrooge's pride got in the way for nearly all of his life, and it was time wasted. Don't let another day go by when pride is holding you back. Let go and find true wisdom that will last for eternity.

Fear of the LORD is the foundation of true knowledge,
but fools despise wisdom and discipline.
PROVERBS 1:7 NLT

THE WORST OF THINGS

The room was very dark, too dark to be observed with any accuracy, though Scrooge glanced round it in obedience to a secret impulse, anxious to know what kind of room it was. A pale light, rising in the outer air, fell straight upon the bed; and on it, plundered and bereft, unwatched, unwept, uncared for, was the body of this man.

Scrooge glanced toward the Phantom. Its steady hand was pointed to the head. The cover was so carelessly adjusted that the slightest raising of it, the motion of a finger upon Scrooge's part, would have disclosed the face. He thought of it, felt how easy it would be to do, and longed to do it, but had not more power to withdraw the veil than to dismiss the specter at his side. . . .

He lay in the dark, empty house, with not a man, a woman, or a child to say he was kind to me in this or that, and for the memory of one kind word I will be kind to him. A cat was tearing at the door, and there was a sound of gnawing rats beneath the hearthstone. What they wanted in the room of death, and why they were so restless and disturbed, Scrooge did not dare to think.

"Spirit!" he said, "this is a fearful place. In leaving it, I shall not leave its lesson, trust me. Let us go!"

Still the Ghost pointed with an unmoved finger to the head.

"I understand you," Scrooge returned, "and I would do it, if I could. But I have not the power, Spirit. I have not the power."

A man has died, that much is certain. But as for the identity of the dead man, Scrooge can't say for sure. The Ghost refuses to answer his questions, and the conversations he has overheard on London's streets regarding the man's death don't provide enough information for Ebenezer to even make a guess. Whoever this dead man is, he seems to be altogether unimportant or a laughingstock to the people who take the time to even mention his passing. No one mourns. No one has fond memories to share of the deceased.

But of course! A realization flashes through Scrooge's mind. The Ghost is showing him an example of some other unhappy man's fate that might be his if he doesn't change his ways.

The Ghost transports the two to a darkened bedroom, completely empty of all bed curtains, blankets, and pillows except for a single dirty sheet wrapped around the man's lifeless body.

The pang of loss, the utter end of lonely existence, the absence of hope, the full weight of a meaningless life hits Scrooge so squarely in the chest that he nearly falls to his knees. No one is there to tend to the man's remains; no one is there to respect the dead. . .except for the cats and rats who eagerly await their next meal.

Scrooge's time with the Ghost of Christmas Future is just beginning, but already we see what an impact it has on him. And rightfully so! Scrooge has lived his life with relatively few consequences so far. He has done just as he pleases, treating people just as he wants to—thinking only of himself and his growing fortune. But now he is facing a reality to which he has never given much thought: death.

Scrooge is on a path for destruction that each of us travel at some point in our lives. That path—a life of sin—separates us from God, and it leads to an eternity apart from Him (2 Thessalonians 1:9). The only outcome from unforgiven sin is death:

For the wages of sin is death. . . (Romans 6:23 NLT)

But the good news—the wonderful, most perfect news that we celebrate every day, but especially on Christmas Day—is that Jesus Christ came to earth and made a way for our sins to be forgiven and removed forever. By dying on the cross as the perfect sacrifice for our wrongdoing, Jesus made it so that death is not the end if we have accepted Him as our Savior:

. . .but the free gift of God is eternal life through Christ Jesus our Lord. (Romans 6:23 NLT)

For Christians, death is a beginning to a brand-new life in Christ! We can live every day with that hope and someday die with that hope.

"I am the resurrection and the life. Anyone who believes in me will live, even after dying. Everyone who lives in me and believes in me will never ever die."
JOHN 11:25–26 NLT

TINY TIM'S LEGACY

"But I think [Father] has walked a little slower than he used, these few last evenings, Mother."

They were very quiet again. At last she said, and in a steady, cheerful voice that only faltered once:

"I have known him walk with—I have known him walk with Tiny Tim upon his shoulder very fast indeed."

"And so have I," cried Peter. "Often."

"And so have I," exclaimed another. So had all.

"But he was very light to carry," she resumed, intent upon her work, "and his father loved him so, that it was no trouble—no trouble. And there is your father at the door!"

She hurried out to meet him, and little Bob in his comforter—he had need of it, poor fellow—came in. His tea was ready for him on the hob, and they all tried who should help him to it most. Then the two young Cratchits got upon his knees, and laid, each child, a little cheek against his face, as if they said, "Don't mind it, father. Don't be grieved!"

Bob was very cheerful with them, and spoke pleasantly to all the family. He looked at the work upon the table, and praised the industry and speed of Mrs. Cratchit and the girls. They would be done long before Sunday, he said.

"Sunday! You went today, then, Robert?" said his wife.

"Yes, my dear," returned Bob. "I wish you could have gone. It would have done you good to see how green a place it is. But you'll see it often. I promised him that

I would walk there on a Sunday. My little, little child!"
cried Bob. "My little child!"

He broke down all at once. He couldn't help it. If he
could have helped it, he and his child would have been
farther apart, perhaps, than they were. . . .

"I am sure we shall none of us forget poor Tiny
Tim—shall we?—or this first parting that there was
among us?"

"Never, Father!" cried they all.

"And I know," said Bob, "I know, my dears, that
when we recollect how patient and how mild he was,
although he was a little, little child, we shall not quarrel
easily among ourselves, and forget poor Tiny Tim in
doing it."

"No, never, father!" they all cried again. "I am very
happy," said little Bob. "I am very happy!" Mrs. Cratchit
kissed him, his daughters kissed him, the two young
Cratchits kissed him, and Peter and himself shook hands.
Spirit of Tiny Tim, thy childish essence was from God!

Tiny Tim Cratchit was full of hope and love until the
very end, but his short life ended much as the doctor
had predicted. The young boy had continued to get weaker,
and in the weeks leading up to Christmas, an infection in
his lungs overtook his entire body. And now the Cratchit
Christmas has one less little soul to add to the festivities.

Bob knows he is a better man for having known and
loved his youngest son. Tim left the world a better place than
he found it, and his loving, gentle spirit will live on in the
Cratchits' hearts and memories forever. Although the loss is

so fresh that Bob feels like he will never be happy, he and his family will laugh again. It's what Tiny Tim would want.

Do you ever feel insignificant, unimportant, unable to make a difference? Maybe because you're young or inexperienced or don't have lots of money, you may think it's useless to make an effort because you can't really do anything.

Take a lesson from Tiny Tim. Dickens doesn't tell us how old Tiny Tim is in the story, but we know he was a young child—most movies and plays cast actors somewhere between the ages of five and eight. That is very few years to make an impact, but make an impact he did.

The Bible encourages us to make a mark for good, no matter our age or importance. God doesn't put requirements on doing good for others, and neither should we.

> *Don't let anyone think less of you because you are young.*
> *Be an example to all believers in what you say, in the*
> *way you live, in your love, your faith, and your purity.*
> *(1 Timothy 4:12 NLT)*

Tiny Tim will be remembered, but unless Scrooge changes his ways, he will not. How are you living your life—as Tiny Tim or as Scrooge? Choose goodness and follow Tiny Tim's example in a life that matters!

> *How can a young person stay pure?*
> *By obeying your word.*
> PSALM 119:9 NLT

SCROOGE'S DEMISE

*A churchyard. . . . The Spirit stood among the graves
and pointed down to one. [Scrooge] advanced toward
it, trembling. The Phantom was exactly as it had been,
but he dreaded that he saw new meaning in its solemn
shape.*

*"Before I draw nearer to that stone to which you
point," said Scrooge, "answer me one question. Are
these the shadows of the things that will be or are they
shadows of the things that may be, only?". . .*

The Spirit was immovable as ever.

*Scrooge crept toward it, trembling as he went; and
following the finger, read upon the stone of the neglected
grave his own name, EBENEZER SCROOGE.*

*"Am I that man who lay upon the bed," he cried,
upon his knees.*

*The finger pointed from the grave to him, and back
again.*

*"No, Spirit! Oh, no, no!" The finger still was there.
"Spirit!" he cried, tight clutching at its robe, "hear me!
I am not the man I was. I will not be the man I must
have been but for this intercourse. Why show me this, if
I am past all hope?" For the first time the hand appeared
to shake.*

*"Good Spirit," he pursued, as down upon the
ground he fell before it, "your nature intercedes for me
and pities me. Assure me that I yet may change these
shadows you have shown me, by an altered life!"*

The kind hand trembled.

"I will honor Christmas in my heart and try to keep

it all the year. I will live in the past, present, and the future. The Spirits of all three shall strive within me. I will not shut out the lessons that they teach. Oh, tell me I may sponge away the writing on this stone!". . .

Holding up his hands in a last prayer to have his fate reversed, he saw an alteration in the Phantom's hood and dress. It shrank, collapsed, and dwindled down into a bedpost.

Scrooge has done his best to deny where the Ghost of Christmas Future would ultimately lead him, but as he stares at the deserted graveyard, the ever-present London fog seems to thicken and swirl all the more. The arm of the Ghost rises to point to one final destination for Scrooge: a grave.

Any hope Ebenezer still holds in his heart that it is someone else's name on the stone quickly shrinks as the Ghost is even more adamant that he look at the stone. There must be a way out. There must be a way to change these terrible things that he has seen. But the large letters on the headstone come into focus as the fog shifts. . .E-B-E-N-E-Z-E-R. . .S-C-R-O-O-G-E.

The picture flashes through Scrooge's head of the dead man, forgotten, unwanted, wrapped in a sheet and left to the animals. He sees Tiny Tim's single crutch leaning in the corner as Bob Cratchit mourns the loss of his beloved son.

But maybe it's not too late.

Scrooge pleads, on his knees, for a second chance from the Ghost—a real and authentic cry of repentance from a man who has never once felt truly sorry in his life. And because Scrooge's heart is beginning to show true change, the

Ghost shows pity on the pitiful man.

All throughout our story, we have seen evidence that Scrooge is a man who is beyond all hope. After decades of developing a heart of stone and treating others absolutely terribly, hatefully, unjustly, and unfairly, it may have been impossible to imagine redemption for such a person. But the truth wrapped up in Christmas for Scrooge is that there *is* hope.

God is faithful to forgive even the worst among us—the real Scrooges of this earth—if we are willing to admit that we need His forgiveness:

> *If we claim we have no sin, we are only fooling ourselves and not living in the truth. But if we confess our sins to him, he is faithful and just to forgive us our sins and to cleanse us from all wickedness. (1 John 1:8–9 NLT)*

Who do you know who needs this hope? Eternal hope came to the world wrapped in swaddling clothes, sleeping in a trough for animal food. Jesus Christ is the reason we can live lives of love that make a difference now and for eternity. Celebrate by sharing that hope this Christmas!

As for me, I will always have hope;
I will praise you more and more.
PSALM 71:14 NIV

Stave Five

LIVING IN THE PAST,
PRESENT, AND FUTURE

Yes! And the bedpost was his own. The bed was his own, the room was his own. Best and happiest of all, the time before him was his own, to make amends in!

"I will live in the past, the present, and the future!" Scrooge repeated, as he scrambled out of bed. "The Spirits of all three shall strive within me. O Jacob Marley! Heaven and the Christmastime be praised for this! I say it on my knees, old Jacob, on my knees!"

He was so fluttered and so glowing with his good intentions, that his broken voice would scarcely answer to his call. He had been sobbing violently in his conflict with the Spirit, and his face was wet with tears.

"They are not torn down," cried Scrooge, folding one of his bed-curtains in his arms—"they are not torn down, rings and all. They are here—I am here—the shadows of the things that would have been may be dispelled. They will be. I know they will!"

His hands were busy with his garments all this time; turning them inside out, putting them on upside down, tearing them, mislaying them, making them parties to every kind of extravagance.

"I don't know what to do!" cried Scrooge, laughing and crying in the same breath. . . . "I am as light as a feather, I am as happy as an angel, I am as merry as a schoolboy. I am as giddy as a drunken man. A merry Christmas to everybody! A happy New Year to all the world! Hallo here! Whoop! Hallo!"

As the graveyard melts away, Scrooge finds himself transported back to his bedchamber, just as he left it. He inhales a deep breath, feeling life in his lungs, and thanks Heaven for a second chance—even offering thanks for the haunting visit he had received from Jacob Marley that now feels like a lifetime ago.

Ebenezer Scrooge has always prided himself in knowing exactly what to do in any circumstance, but right now he doesn't have a single notion of what to do first. So his tears of anguish change to tears of joy, and he marvels at the fact that the bed curtains that he had recently seen torn down were now perfectly intact. The shadows that haunted him are gone, and he can begin again—his new life awaits!

Do you remember when you began your life new in Christ? We each have different stories about who we were before we knew Jesus, how He changed our lives, and who we are now, living in His salvation. Our story may not be as dramatic as Scrooge's, but scripture tells us that the power of God's grace changes us.

> *Therefore, if anyone is in Christ, the new creation has come: The old has gone, the new is here! All this is from God, who reconciled us to himself through Christ and gave us the ministry of reconciliation: that God was reconciling the world to himself in Christ, not counting people's sins against them. And he has committed to us the message of reconciliation. (2 Corinthians 5:17–19 NIV)*

Scrooge happily announces that he will live in the past, present, and future. For the first time in his life, Scrooge is looking at his life more broadly and considering the roles that other people play in his story. We, too, can learn from all three. Our past (sin) shapes us, our present (repentance) changes us, and our future (salvation), gives us hope to live every day in God's powerful love. God has such wonderful plans for His children, and just like Scrooge, we can live out that plan every day of our lives, starting today.

Don't let another minute go by. Whether you have been a Christian for years or you have yet to accept the forgiveness of God, don't wait to take the next step in your faith walk. Let God change your heart, and watch as you're changed into an entirely new creation!

I forget everything that is behind me and look forward to that which is ahead of me. My eyes are on the crown. I want to win the race and get the crown of God's call from heaven through Christ Jesus.
PHILIPPIANS 3:13–14 NLV

TRUE CELEBRATION

[Scrooge] had frisked into the sitting room and was now standing there, perfectly winded. "There's the saucepan that the gruel was in!" cried Scrooge, starting off again, and going round the fireplace.

"There's the door by which the Ghost of Jacob Marley entered! There's the corner where the Ghost of Christmas Present sat! There's the window where I saw the wandering Spirits! It's all right, it's all true, it all happened. Ha, ha, ha!"

Really, for a man who had been out of practice for so many years, it was a splendid laugh, a most illustrious laugh. The father of a long, long line of brilliant laughs!

"I don't know what day of the month it is," said Scrooge. "I don't know how long I have been among the Spirits. I don't know anything. I'm quite a baby. Never mind. I don't care. I'd rather be a baby. Hallo! Whoop! Hallo here!"

He was checked in his transports by the churches ringing out the lustiest peals he had ever heard. Clash, clash, hammer; ding, dong, bell! Bell, dong, ding; hammer, clang, clash! Oh, glorious, glorious!

Running to the window, he opened it and put out his head. No fog, no mist; clear, bright, jovial, stirring, cold; cold, piping for the blood to dance to; golden sunlight; heavenly sky; sweet fresh air; merry bells. Oh, glorious! Glorious!

Scrooge quickly dresses and sprints like a man half his age to his sitting room, where he finds the remnants of last night's gruel sitting on the cold hearth. Scrooge tries to catch his breath through great gulps of air between expressions of utter excitement. You'd think that the saucepan was the most joyous site Ebenezer had ever seen—as if the gruel were a long-lost, beloved relative. Memories of the previous night flood to his mind as he gleefully points out the door that Jacob Marley entered, the place where the Ghost of Christmas Present sat, and the window where he first saw the sky full of spirits that warned him of his fate.

With all that he has learned from the Ghosts, Scrooge wouldn't be surprised if he had been gone for a week. But what time is it? The church bells begin to ring a sweet melody unlike anything Scrooge has ever heard. He throws open the windows to see a crystal-clear morning. Brisk and rejuvenating cold fills Scrooge with such emotion that it bubbles up from his toes in a laugh that reaches his rooftop, sending a nest of pigeons fluttering away in surprise. What a glorious morning! What a blessed life!

Scrooge's response to the seemingly mundane objects around him are like a child's reaction on Christmas morning. Socks become stockings filled with special treats. A pine tree exactly like the ones out in the yard takes on a magical appearance with a strand of lights and a few homemade ornaments. Everything is amazing and perfect and wonderful.

Do you want to experience this kind of joy this Christmas? Scrooge has just gone through a life-changing— an eternity-changing—experience, and his celebration is pure and true. And our Christmas celebration as Christians can be just as wondrous and exciting if we focus on the true meaning of the holiday.

Think of it! God's perfect plan included a way for us to become new, holy, perfect, accepted sons and daughters of the King. Even before the world knew of Jesus' arrival, the angels gave the shepherds a preview of the excitement:

The angel said to them, "Do not be afraid. I bring you good news that will cause great joy for all the people. Today in the town of David a Savior has been born to you; he is the Messiah, the Lord." (Luke 2:10–11 NIV)

God, in His great love, made a way for us to be with Him, and we don't have to be haunted by three Spirits. We don't have to see our ultimate demise as Scrooge did with the Ghost of Christmas Future. All we have to do is accept His gift of salvation, and then celebrate! Celebrate this day and every day, knowing that the hope, joy, and peace that bless your heart are gifts straight from heaven (Romans 15:13). Today is the day that God has made—so rejoice (Psalm 118:24)!

May the God of hope fill you with all joy and peace as you trust in him, so that you may overflow with hope by the power of the Holy Spirit.
ROMANS 15:13 NIV

SECRET BLESSINGS

"What's today?" cried Scrooge, calling downward to a boy in Sunday clothes, who perhaps had loitered in to look about him.

"Eh?" returned the boy, with all his might of wonder.

"What's today, my fine fellow?" said Scrooge.

"Today!" replied the boy. "Why, Christmas Day."

"It's Christmas Day!" said Scrooge to himself. "I haven't missed it. The Spirits have done it all in one night. They can do anything they like. Of course they can. Of course they can. Hallo, my fine fellow!"

"Hallo!" returned the boy.

"Do you know the poulterer's, in the next street but one, at the corner?" Scrooge inquired.

"I should hope I did," replied the lad.

"An intelligent boy!" said Scrooge. "A remarkable boy! Do you know whether they've sold the prize turkey that was hanging up there?—Not the little prize turkey, the big one?"

"What, the one as big as me?" returned the boy.

"What a delightful boy!" said Scrooge. "It's a pleasure to talk to him. Yes, my buck! . . . Go and buy it, and tell 'em to bring it here, that I may give them the directions where to take it. Come back with the man, and I'll give you a shilling. Come back with him in less than five minutes, and I'll give you half a crown!"

The boy was off like a shot. He must have had a steady hand at a trigger who could have got a shot off half so fast.

"I'll send it to Bob Cratchit's," whispered Scrooge, rubbing his hands and splitting with a laugh. "He shan't know who sends it. It's twice the size of Tiny Tim."

s Scrooge admires the sparkling snow on the London rooftops, movement on the street below catches his eye. A small boy, dressed in his Sunday finest, walks along the street whistling a Christmas carol. Scrooge calls out to him to ask what day it is.

The boy wonders if the man is crazy or is just playing a joke. It's the most wonderful day of the year—Christmas Day!

It is the answer Scrooge secretly hoped it would be! The Spirits had done it all in one night! Ebenezer claps in delight and shifts his focus on the first task at hand—a bird for the Cratchits' Christmas feast. But not just any bird—the prize turkey (twice as big as Tiny Tim) in the butcher's window. And this lad in the street is the perfect person to take care of the errand.

With his mission in hand and Scrooge's promise of a generous tip, the boy runs in the direction of the shop, quite unsure of exactly what is going on. Old Mr. Scrooge seems to have lost his marbles once and for all, and if nothing else, this will make a great story to tell his family.

But Ebenezer Scrooge's marbles and heart are not lost. It has been years since his mind has been this clear. He will make things right with his clerk tomorrow, but today—the Cratchits will eat like kings!

If we still need evidence that Scrooge has truly experienced a transformation, the fact that the very first thought (once he gets his bearings and finds out what day it is) is to bless others on Christmas Day—namely, the Cratchit family.

Whether Scrooge knew it or not, he did his very first act of generosity the way God asks us to give in scripture:

"Watch out! Don't do your good deeds publicly, to be admired by others, for you will lose the reward from your Father in heaven. When you give to someone in

*need, don't do as the hypocrites do—blowing trumpets
in the synagogues and streets to call attention to their
acts of charity! I tell you the truth, they have received
all the reward they will ever get. But when you give to
someone in need, don't let your left hand know what
your right hand is doing. Give your gifts in private,
and your Father, who sees everything, will reward you."*
(Matthew 6:1–4 NLT)

True giving and selfless generosity don't need admirers. They don't need the receiver of the blessing to write a thank-you note or to praise the giver. When we give from a pure heart, we know that God is glorified in our actions, and that is a reward in and of itself.

This Christmas look for ways to give personally and anonymously. Maybe you could give through an angel tree project that provides Christmas gifts for needy children, or perhaps you could provide a Christmas meal for a family you know. Fill a box with the makings of a Christmas feast, put a bow on it, leave it on the front porch, ring the doorbell, and run! Secrets are fun, especially at Christmas, and giving generously toward real needs is a wonderful way to celebrate the season with your family.

*Make the most of every opportunity
in these evil days. Don't act thoughtlessly,
but understand what the Lord wants you to do.*
EPHESIANS 5:16–17 NLT

CHRISTMAS FORGIVENESS

[Scrooge] passed the door a dozen times before he had the courage to go up and knock. But he made a dash and did it.

"Is your master at home, my dear?" said Scrooge to the girl. Nice girl! Very.

"Yes, sir."

"Where is he, my love?" said Scrooge.

"He's in the dining room, sir, along with mistress. I'll show you upstairs, if you please."

"Thankee. He knows me," said Scrooge, with his hand already on the dining room lock. "I'll go in here, my dear."

He turned it gently, and sidled his face in round the door. They were looking at the table (which was spread out in great array); for these young housekeepers are always nervous on such points and like to see that everything is right.

"Fred!" said Scrooge.

Dear heart alive, how his niece by marriage started! Scrooge had forgotten, for the moment, about her sitting in the corner with the footstool, or he wouldn't have done it on any account.

"Why, bless my soul!" cried Fred, "who's that?"

"It's I. Your uncle Scrooge. I have come to dinner. Will you let me in, Fred?"

Let him in! It is a mercy he didn't shake his arm off. He was at home in five minutes. Nothing could be heartier. His niece looked just the same. . . . Wonderful party, wonderful games, wonderful unanimity, wonderful happiness!

The old Ebenezer Scrooge never would have expected to find himself knocking on his nephew's door—especially on Christmas Day—but the new Ebenezer Scrooge knows it's where he wants to be. All the same, excited nerves bubble so in his stomach that working up the courage to knock on the door is terribly difficult.

What if Fred dismisses him? The young man would have every right to do so. Or worse, what if Fred and his lovely wife laugh in the old man's face? The very thought nearly has Scrooge turning on a heel and walking back to his house. But the door opens at just that moment, and the sweet face and cheery "Merry Christmas" from the maid give him the courage to do what he has come to do.

"Fred!" At Scrooge's greeting, his nephew whirls around and nearly drops his teacup and saucer. His mouth open in shock, he glances at his wife sitting in the corner, whose eyes were nearly as big as the saucer teetering in Fred's hand. *As if they've seen a ghost*, Scrooge chuckles to himself.

Scrooge fiddles with his cuff links as he stumbles with the question he has come to ask. He casts a nervous glance at Fred, who seems to have collected himself after the initial shock of seeing his uncle, and the man smiles back warmly. Scrooge clears his throat and asks a question full of hope and repentance: "Will you allow me to come to Christmas dinner, nephew?"

Before Scrooge can get the whole question out, Fred is already pumping his arm in a hearty handshake. Fred's misty-eyed wife kisses Scrooge on his weather-worn cheek, and the uncle lets out a sigh of relief. He knows he is home for Christmas.

Asking for forgiveness may seem like a simple thing. If

we do something wrong and it affects others, admitting that we're sorry and that we did not mean to hurt them is a pretty cut-and-dried interaction. But there are lots of other details that can make asking for forgiveness difficult—like if we let our pride get in the way. Another problem is time. The longer we let unforgiveness go, the harder it is to approach someone and ask for it. Scrooge knew he had mistreated his nephew perhaps all his life, so it's no wonder that he paused slightly at the door.

But the truth is that God wants us to work toward forgiveness whenever it is necessary. Whether you are the person who needs forgiveness or the person who needs to forgive, take a lesson from Scrooge's story and put the past behind and look forward to a future of peace. Doing that honors what God tells us to do in Hebrews 12:

> *Work at living in peace with everyone, and work at living a holy life, for those who are not holy will not see the Lord. (verse 14 NLT)*

Don't wait for the "perfect" time to ask for forgiveness. Today is the perfect time. Live at peace with others and you will experience the true peace of Christmas this year.

You should be kind to others and have no pride. Be gentle and be willing to wait for others. Try to understand other people. Forgive each other. If you have something against someone, forgive him. That is the way the Lord forgave you.
COLOSSIANS 3:12–13 NLV

SURPRISE GENEROSITY

But [Scrooge] was early at the office next morning, Oh, he was early there! If he could only be there first, and catch Bob Cratchit coming late! That was the thing he had set his heart upon.

And he did it, yes, he did! The clock struck nine. No Bob. A quarter past. No Bob. He was full eighteen minutes and a half behind his time. Scrooge sat with his door wide open, that he might see him come into the tank.

His hat was off before he opened the door, his comforter, too. He was on his stool in a jiffy, driving away with his pen, as if he were trying to overtake nine o'clock.

"Hallo!" growled Scrooge, in his accustomed voice as near as he could feign it. "What do you mean by coming here at this time of day?"

"I am very sorry, sir," said Bob. "I am behind my time."

"You are?" repeated Scrooge. "Yes. I think you are. Step this way, sir, if you please."

"It's only once a year, sir," pleaded Bob, appearing from the tank. "It shall not be repeated. I was making rather merry yesterday, sir."

"Now, I'll tell you what, my friend," said Scrooge, "I am not going to stand this sort of thing any longer. And therefore," he continued, leaping from his stool and giving Bob such a dig in the waistcoat that he staggered back into the tank again—"and therefore, I am about to raise your salary!"

Bob trembled and got a little nearer to the ruler. He

had a momentary idea of knocking Scrooge down with it, holding him, and calling to the people in the court for help and a strait-waistcoat.

"A merry Christmas, Bob!" said Scrooge, with an earnestness that could not be mistaken, as he clapped him on the back. "A merrier Christmas, Bob, my good fellow, than I have given you for many a year! I'll raise your salary, and endeavor to assist your struggling family, and we will discuss your affairs this very afternoon, over a Christmas bowl of smoking bishop, Bob! Make up the fires and buy another coal scuttle before you dot another i, Bob Cratchit!"

Bob Cratchit's belly was still so contented from the giant leftover turkey wing he had eaten last night that he slept in a full thirty minutes this morning. Christmas had been such a lovely day. Never in Bob's life had he eaten so much food, and there had been no need for rationing yesterday. Tiny Tim had even gotten his very own turkey leg, which was longer and rounder than the boy's arm, and gleefully devoured meat off the bone.

But now poor Bob would have to own up to his tardiness and take whatever punishment Mr. Scrooge chose to dole out. The clerk rushes into the Scrooge & Marley office a full eighteen minutes late, and Scrooge looks like he is ready to launch into a screaming fit that is sure to end in Bob's dismissal.

"I'm not going to stand for this sort of thing any longer. . . ." Bob feels his face warm in embarrassment (or is it actually warmer than normal in the office?). He tries to focus on the ledger in front of him as Mr. Scrooge's voice gets louder with each word. Here it comes. At least the Cratchits had one truly bountiful and joyous Christmas together.

". . .raise your salary!"

Bob shakes his head slightly, wondering if the cobwebs of sleep are still clogging up his brain. What did Mr. Scrooge say? And why is he grinning like a cat that swallowed the canary? Has the old man finally cracked? Bob eyes the ruler sitting on the edge of his desk, wondering if he can work up the nerve to use it in self-defense if he needs to.

But Mr. Scrooge's countenance isn't that of a crazy person, and now he is wishing Bob a merry Christmas with every sincerity. A larger paycheck! Help for the family! More coal for the office fires! Scrooge takes such glee in explaining these points to Bob that even though he can't fathom it all, he heartily shakes his employer's hand and joins in the celebration.

All of the changes Scrooge has experienced so far have been leading up to this point in the story, when he gives—extravagantly—to Bob and his family. It's not just a larger paycheck that Scrooge gives Bob, it's a promise to be there for the family and to make a personal investment in them, to help them however they might need him. Scrooge (with the help of the Ghosts) has opened up his eyes and heart to understand the real struggle that the Cratchits deal with on a daily basis, and through Scrooge's transformation, it's obvious to him where he can make a real difference.

It may have been a lifetime in coming, but Ebenezer is finally experiencing the joy of giving. Very likely Scrooge will continue to be a hard worker, and he will probably continue to make vast amounts of money, but in his new life he will find great happiness in giving much of his wealth away to people who need it. He is living out what scripture tells us to do in Acts 20:

> *"I have been a constant example of how you can help those in need by working hard. You should remember the words of the Lord Jesus: 'It is more blessed to give than to receive.'" (verse 35 NLT)*

Until now, Scrooge never would have believed Jesus' words here. The world tells us that getting is so much better than giving, but Christ's kingdom is an upside-down kingdom. Work hard all year to earn, and then give this Christmas and every day—and be blessed!

> *Tell them to use their money to do good. They should be rich in good works and generous to those in need, always being ready to share with others. By doing this they will be storing up their treasure as a good foundation for the future so that they may experience true life.*
> 1 TIMOTHY 6:18–19 NLT

CONCLUSION

Scrooge was better than his word. He did it all, and infinitely more; and to Tiny Tim, who did not die, he was a second father. He became as good a friend, as good a master, and as good a man as the good old city knew, or any other good old city, town, or borough in the good old world. Some people laughed to see the alteration in him, but he let them laugh and little heeded them, for he was wise enough to know that nothing ever happened on this globe for good at which some people did not have their fill of laughter in the outset; and knowing that such as these would be blind anyway, he thought it quite as well that they should wrinkle up their eyes in grins, as have the malady in less attractive forms. His own heart laughed, and that was quite enough for him.

. . .It was always said of him, that he knew how to keep Christmas well, if any man alive possessed the knowledge. May that be truly said of us, and all of us! And so, as Tiny Tim observed,

God bless us, every one!

Scripture Index

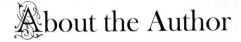About the Author

Annie Tipton made up her first story at the ripe old age of two when she asked her mom to write it down for her. (Hey, she was just two—she didn't know how to make letters yet!) Since then she has read and written many words as a student, newspaper reporter, author, and editor. Annie loves snow (which is a good thing, because she lives in Ohio), wearing scarves, eating sushi, playing Scrabble, and spending time with friends and family.